Essential
Orlando and
Walt Disney World

by
LINDSAY HUNT

Lindsay Hunt turned to travel journalism after a career in publishing and a year sampling tapas in S̶p̶a̶i̶n̶ She has researched many destinations for *Holida̶y̶ ̶w̶h̶i̶c̶h̶?* magazine, and is co-author of several hotel g̶u̶i̶d̶e̶s̶ ̶and a book on Spain.

Produced by AA Publishing

Written by Lindsay Hunt
Peace and Quiet section
by Paul Sterry
Series Adviser: Ingrid Morgan
Copy Editor: Ron Hawkins

Edited, designed and produced
by AA Publishing. Maps ©
The Automobile Association 1993

Distributed in the United Kingdom
by AA Publishing, Fanum House,
Basingstoke, Hampshire,
RG21 2EA.

A CIP catalogue record for this
book is available from the British
Library.

ISBN 0 7495 0518 4

Published by the Automobile
Association.

This book was produced using
QuarkXPress™, Aldus
Freehand™ and Microsoft
Word™ on Apple Macintosh™
computers.

Colour separation: by BTB Colour
Reproduction Ltd, Whitchurch,
Hampshire

Printed by: Printers Trento S.R.L.,
Italy

*Front cover picture: Parade
through Main Street USA,
Walt Disney World.*

Contents

This book employs a simple rating system to help choose which places to visit:

 'top ten' theme parks

◆◆◆ do not miss
◆◆ see if you can
◆ worth seeing if you have time

Introduction and Background

INTRODUCTION

The Florida package suggests glamorous beach-life, national parks, fragile ecosystems, and flourishing orange groves. Not much of this applies to Orlando. Sunshine? Mmm, a bit sultry. Cool it with a coastal breeze on that soft white sand around the Keys. Scenery, then? Central Florida's countryside is fairly uninteresting – flat, lots of unsightly urban sprawl, trailer homes, scrubby pines and withered orange trees. Head south for the Everglades if you are interested in natural habitats. Peace and quiet, a get-away-from-it-all holiday? Absolutely not – are you crazy?

So what is all the hype about this strange boom town in the middle of failed citrus groves? Answer, theme parks. This is definitely the main reason for visiting Orlando on holiday. Not sure you are so keen on theme parks? Then

consider this. If you have never seen Orlando, you have never seen theme parks. These are the biggest, brightest, brassiest of their kind, anywhere in the world. They are on a scale you cannot imagine.

Biggest of all is the Walt Disney World resort, almost as big as San Francisco (twice the size of Manhattan), and still growing with mesmerising speed, engulfing the whole region like some giant bubble. If it ever bursts, the effects will be shattering for the local economy. Walt Disney World is not *all* of Orlando by any means, but it is definitely the focal point. You cannot possibly visit this part of the USA and not see WDW.

There are those who gnash their teeth over Disney and his fellow theme-parkers, accusing them of reducing the universe to 'a sickening blend of cheap formulas packaged to sell', where life is mediocre, blandly safe, and trivially happy. Walt Disney World appeals to children of all ages, but it is Peter Pan land. Here fairy tales are stripped of Grimmer aspects or nasty Freudian connotations, while mermaids are decently covered up with bra-tops.

If today's mass culture of television and computerised technology appalls you, if you prefer to nourish your children on a diet of improving books, Orlando may not be for you. But only the most puritanical believe an occasional hamburger will ruin your life for ever. And that is what Orlando is like – an enormous plateful of the most calorific, imaginative, appetising junk food you will ever taste.

High-quality junk too, however much a contradiction in terms that sounds. Orlando's theme parks, strongly influenced by Walt Disney World, have their own brand of classiness. It exists in their cleanliness, their spick-and-span tidiness, the rigorous standards of maintenance everywhere. Anyone used to less efficient regimes will marvel at the speed and skill with which such vast numbers of people can be moved about, as well as at the courteous and considerate way in which it is done. You will have to queue in Orlando's theme parks (a lot!), but you will not feel

INTRODUCTION

Mickey Mouse

Imaginative design at Orlando extends to the skyline

herded, as tourists so often are. Those cheerful, ever-smiling staff (the 'cast', in Disney parlance) know how to make you, the guest, top dog (visitors are always called 'guests' at WDW, never 'customers'). Litter, disorder, negligence, surliness – these deficiencies are not part of Orlando's world. It is salutary to experience this once in a while, and discover just how well things can be done.

Walt Disney was responsible for these unprecedented standards of Orlando hospitality, posthumously importing his well-tried theme park formula from that other Orange County in California. Outside Walt Disney World there may be people who do *not* wish you a nice day – indeed, a few who plainly could not care less whether you have one or not. Some visitors prefer this closer approximation to the real world to the never-never land of The Magic Kingdom. But the contrast may make you realise, and appreciate, just how much effort those Disney folk put into smiling at you.

Would *you* enjoy Orlando? There is no absolute guarantee, but if you ask the millions who flood through those turnstiles each year if they did enjoy it, most of them say yes, sometimes rather to their surprise.

BACKGROUND

For many visitors, Orlando means Walt Disney
World. Hardly surprising, since WDW is the
most popular man-made tourist destination on
earth. It is now more than 20 years since the
Mouse arrived in Florida from his first theme
park home in Disneyland, California. Things
have changed so rapidly in the area since then
that few can remember what life was like in
those olden days. Disney was by no means the
first theme-parker in Orlando. There were a
number of attractions all doing just fine before
Walt Disney World swung Florida's centre of
gravity firmly inland from the coastal regions.
Disney's most significant rival in Orlando today
is Anheuser–Busch, the brewers of Budweiser
and Michelob, who own three major attractions
in the area (Sea World, Cypress Gardens and
Busch Gardens). The arrival of Universal
Studios from Hollywood in direct competition
with Disney–MGM Studios has also put Walt
Disney World on its mettle. But few would deny
Disney's pre-eminence in Orlando. It is the
sun; other theme parks are mere planets.
In 1970, the year before WDW opened, only
five per cent of Florida's tourists bothered to
visit the central plains. Today it is something
over a third. Some of the older attractions, such
as the Cypress Gardens, are still going strong,
albeit with drastic improvements and
renovations. Others, like Boardwalk and
Baseball, have succumbed to competition,
caught in the slipstream of Disney's
unstoppable juggernaut. The lakes and springs
north and west of Orlando provide popular
recreational lungs for outdoor types.
Florida's coastal magnets still draw hordes, but
overdevelopment and the rising crime rate
have done much to dent the former popularity
of the Gold Coast. Although some parts of
Miami are very attractive, other areas are
dangerous, and some of the coastal
developments are very ugly.
So what is it like, this central belt of the
Sunshine State? Scenically, no great shakes. It
is very flat, with stands of slash pines and
scrubland marking uncultivated ground,
though just north of the Orlando area you will

*Disney's Big
Thunder Mountain*

Hollywood, WDW

find the central highlands, part of the Ocala rock ridge. Lakes, rivers and springs indicate how surprisingly waterlogged this hot region is: the mosquito-infested swamps where alligators skulk in the reedbeds have not yet all been drained. Before the theme park era, when cattle-ranching was one of Florida's economic mainstays, alligators were a serious hazard to young or sick livestock. The cowhands (locally known as 'crackers') learned, the hard way, how to deal with these dim-witted but dangerous reptiles. Alligators are now a lucrative source of income, and are farmed for their attractively mottled skins. Ironically, it is sometimes the former crackers who tend them, wrestling with their vice-like jaws in muddy ditches to entertain passing tourists.

Florida's other economic miracle, of course, is oranges. A vast proportion of the world's concentrated citrus juice is produced here, though most of the successful farms lie south of Orlando, where blight and frost have wreaked havoc among the local groves. Walt Disney's father once had an unsuccessful shot at growing oranges in Florida. Perhaps Walt's decision to buy up that huge chunk of central Florida and turn it into gold was some subconscious filial vengeance on the land that refused to grant his father a decent living. Wherever you drive around Orlando, you will see the sad, withered skeletons of orange trees killed in the last big freeze. Some farmers have doggedly replanted; others have turned to less sensitive plants like strawberries and sweetcorn, or to tourism. But Walt Disney World's address is Orange County, Florida, and evermore shall be so.

Orlando, the seat of Orange County, covers a vast, sprawling metropolitan area across three counties, and is still rapidly expanding, with immigration currently running at something like 1,000 new residents a week. About a quarter of its inhabitants make a living from tourism. Its permanent population is about a million, but it is annually inundated by around 14 times that number of tourists, who obviously contribute vast profits (something like $4.6 billion in 1989) to its coffers, and in return

Re-creating the American dream

place huge strains on its resources. The potential for ecological damage caused by Orlando's booming tourism industry is only just dawning, and scientists are casting very anxious eyes on the Everglades National Park, where most of Orlando's industrial and domestic pollution eventually winds up. Walt Disney's touching faith in technological progress as a universally Good Thing would take a few knocks were he still alive today. Before Disney, the Orlando area had around 6,000 hotel rooms. Now it has something like 80,000 (which is more than New York!), with more to come. Disney owns and operates about 12 per cent of these. The Walt Disney World resort has about 33,000 permanent staff, and is by far the biggest employer in central Florida. After US visitors, the largest group of tourists in recent years has come from Britain, followed by rapidly increasing numbers from Latin America.

Besides Walt Disney World, the Orlando area has received much publicity and a considerable amount of associated industrial development from its proximity to Cape Canaveral, launch-pad of the US space programme since the 1960s.

Orlando now hosts an enormous slice of the USA's lucrative convention (conference) market (many of its hotels are specifically geared for that), and many large companies have moved their head offices here. In comparison with other parts of Florida, particularly Miami, its population is young and sprightly, fully able to take advantage of the area's remarkable range of sports and outdoor amenities.

Orlando is an undistinguished place, though not unpleasant or dangerous compared with some large American cities. A few bits of older architecture have been saved (or more accurately, carefully reproduced) to amuse tourists, but these scarcely form integral parts of the modern city, and now seem as artificial as its theme park attractions. There is little reason to venture downtown and explore, still less to stay in the city centre; the most you are likely to see is a few high-rises as you bypass the city on Interstate Highway 4, or the areas

BACKGROUND

Just one of many pavilions at EPCOT

that you pass through on the way to its few central sights, such as Church Street Station. Most of the metropolitan area merges into an ugly mishmash of billboards, shopping malls, motels and gas stations, with multi-lane highways stretching in all directions. An exception is the pleasant northerly residential district of Winter Park, perhaps the only place in Orlando you might go to for its intrinsic appeal.

Historically, Orlando's pedigree amounts to little more than an encampment for soldiers fighting the Seminole Indian War at the beginning of the 19th century. The name is alleged to refer to one Orlando Reeves, a scout who spied a log rolling suspiciously towards him one night while on watch, fired at it, and thus saved his fellow campers from an untimely ambush by Indians. The unfortunate Orlando, however, was killed by the arrow the 'log' had already launched at him. The city was officially given its present name in 1857.

Most of Orlando's attractions lie southwest of the city, easily reached via Interstate Highway 4, the most useful road artery in the area. All the life-support systems tourists need are within this area, and the Walt Disney World resort is completely self-contained, like a space station on some distant planet. It barely seems to interact with its neighbourhood at all – a deliberate policy. Walt Disney did his best to keep the outside world and its undesirable influences at bay, not wishing to make the same mistake he had with Disneyland in California, now besieged by hideous urban sprawl. Walt wanted his new Magic Kingdom to sustain the illusions he conjured into it. Once within Walt Disney World's Maingate, you enter another world. When you leave its confines, you may well see Walt's point.

EPCOT's Spaceship Earth and the monorail

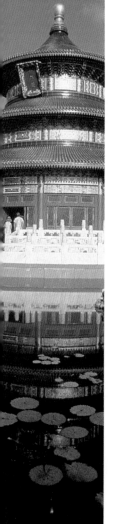

Old Peking under
Orlando skies

Walt Disney – The Dreamfinder

In EPCOT Center there is a ride called Journey into Imagination. It is not one of WDW's best efforts, but its theme would probably have appealed a lot to Walt. In it an adventurer called Dreamfinder erratically pilots a strange flying machine on a quest for new ideas, eternally optimistic about future progress. Not unlike Disney himself.

Successful tycoons come and go, but few have captured so many imaginations, influenced so many people, aroused such controversy, such passionate loyalties and loathings, and such enormous interest, as Walt Disney. Journalists devote years to analysing his life and work; articles and books proliferate on the subject of his empire, weighing its benign or malignant influences. Walt Disney has been dead for over 25 years, yet through the huge and vastly powerful organisation he set in motion he has achieved an alarming degree of immortality. Mickey Mouse, his most memorable creation, is now over 60 years old, but in his bright new coating he looks set to outlive any number of ephemeral Turtles or Muppets. In a survey asking people to name the top ten Americans most successful in business, Walt Disney came second only to Henry Ford, and way ahead of those awesome heroes Carnegie and Rockefeller.

Walter Elias Disney came from humble origins, his father a struggling Mid-Westerner whose varied enterprises consistently failed. When they did, he upped sticks and moved his wife and their five children to pastures new. Walt had a scrappy education, and spent his spare time living on his wits, selling newspapers on street corners, hawking sodas on trains, painting camouflage helmets, and discovering a marked if not outstanding talent for drawing. The family had moved to Kansas City, and it was here, in 1920, that Walt decided to try his hand at cartoon shorts and advertisements. Within three years he was bankrupt. Walt, undaunted, went to Hollywood and, after many false starts and financial failures, achieved some sort of a living in animated silent cartoons, in partnership with his elder brother Roy.

BACKGROUND

The backlot,
Universal Studios

Losing control of his most successful cartoon character, Oswald the Rabbit, to an unprincipled New York distributor taught Walt a lesson he never forgot about trusting people. Walt, thoroughly down on his luck and wiped out of cash, began idly doodling on the long train journey from New York back to Hollywood – or so the story goes. The rough outline took shape somewhere in Ohio or Kansas. It was a mouse.

Mickey's success developed gradually over many years. He acquired a circle of friends – Donald Duck, Goofy, Pluto – and enabled the Disney brothers to set up a new studio, Walt Disney Productions.

Roy Disney tried to temper Walt's wilder impulses with notes of sensible financial caution, but Walt, always cavalier about the money side of things, was the enthusiast, the ideas man, a huge risk-taker, a born entrepreneur. If he did not have the necessary artistic gifts to make the most of the exciting new cinematic technology, he knew a man who did, and slowly the Disney empire began to prosper, with blockbusting, full-length feature animations like *Snow White*, *Pinocchio* and *Fantasia*.

From full-length animations Walt tried his hand at live-action historical adventure films, comedies and wildlife pictures. *Davy Crockett* and *Mary Poppins* contributed vastly to the Disney coffers. The core of the business was always good, clean, family entertainment for those post-war baby boomers. With enormous prescience, the Disneys seized the opportunities presented by the new era of television, while fellow cinema moguls crumbled before the small screen.

Above all, Walt was a weaver of stories (and a shameless borrower of them), by all accounts a gifted raconteur and a brilliant editor. All his life he worked absurdly, obsessively hard, even coming dangerously close to a nervous breakdown in 1931. When they arrived in the mornings his staff would find little notes on blue paper waiting to inform them about wilted flowers or burned-out light bulbs, the result of Walt's nocturnal wanderings to exercise his passion for order and neatness. He led an exemplary settled and happy domestic life with his wife and two daughters – and a miniature steam train in the back garden. Walt first dreamt of amusement parks in the 1930s, but it was not until the 1950s that his obsession developed fully. Amusement parks and circuses at that stage were fairly tacky and disreputable places, and Walt had great difficulty communicating his dream of a place of fun and fantasy in a tidy, orderly setting. His visions went far beyond fairground thrill rides; he wanted *themes* that reinforced his faith in technological progress and the future, a sanitised, deathless world where evil could never triumph, and the archetypal American virtues of pluck and innocence could flourish. Roy refused to let Walt have the money for Disneyland; he had to cash in his life insurance policy to set it up. But when he turned his attention to Florida there was no such hesitancy about the $5.5 million or so (a mere fleabite to Disney by then) to purchase the land. Walt had proved his point: his theme parks were a different order of magnitude from anyone else's. They represented his ideal private universe.

*EPCOT's
Caribbean
Beach Resort*

BACKGROUND

The geosphere looms over EPCOT

The Making of Walt Disney World

The founder of this spectacular pleasure park never lived to see it completed. Disney selected the site for three reasons: large tracts of land were available cheaply, the Orlando area was already booming, and it stood at the crossroads of several major traffic arteries. Perhaps, also, the name augured well: Disneyland had prospered in Orange County, California; now here was Orange County, Florida, ripe for picking. Disney deliberately turned his back on Florida's popular coast, but his apparently eccentric decision to put a theme park in the middle of nowhere paid off. Walt wanted people to visit his man-made phenomenon, not be sidetracked by natural wonders such as oceans or mountains or national parks. Quietly, without publicity, the land was purchased on behalf of Disney back in 1964, and the bulldozers soon moved in to hack down the palmetto scrub and build drainage canals. Meanwhile, Walt's ambitions for his brave new world grew like beanstalks; he wanted not merely a theme park or holiday resort, but an entire Utopian city, without slums, poverty or crime – a model of successful planning and innovative lifestyles. Sadly, Disney lost his race against time. Uncle Walt's signature tune, a perpetual smoker's cough, suddenly developed a more sinister note in the spring of 1966, and by the end of the year he was dead. At only 65, he was still full of energy and bursting with ideas for his great Floridian dream, which he mapped out on the ceiling from his hospital bed until the day he died. It was left to his heirs and a new-look Team Disney master-minded by brother Roy to construct Walt Disney World from the blueprint. It finally opened in October 1971. Today it has clones, in Tokyo and Paris. Many visitors refer to WDW simply as 'Disney World', after the Californian prototype Disneyland. Walt's elder brother Roy insisted on giving it the founder's tag ('Walt Disney World') after his death, a generous personal tribute to the man who had ignored all Roy's predictions, and trusted his own instincts. Within the Disney organisation, the name is never shortened to 'Disney World'.

THEME PARK TIPS

A few golden rules for enjoying the action-packed offerings of Orlando. These apply to most of the large theme parks in the area, but particularly to Walt Disney World.

● Plan your visits carefully. You will not make the most of Orlando in a limited time unless you have very clear ideas of what you want to do. Prioritise the things that attract you most. Study the theme park maps and guides (freely available from many sources) like a military exercise; most are very clear and helpful. Check park opening times (they may vary at short notice throughout the year depending on demand). Arrive at the large parks early, and pace yourself for a long day.

● Learn to queue creatively! There is a lot of queuing to do. The parks try their best to entertain you as you wait with video shows on monitors above the lines, but there is no avoiding a lot of hanging about for popular attractions.

● Remember where you leave your car. Note the row number or section name. Write it down. (If you do forget, you will get so mad you will never do it again!) Staff are on hand to help if you really get stuck. Never leave pets in cars – they will fry, for even in January the average temperature is over 22°C (70°F).

● Wear cool, comfortable clothes, especially shoes. Take precautions against the sun, even in winter – the Florida sun is very strong, and some

Those ears get everywhere...

people (particularly children and those with fair skins) can get sunburnt in half an hour or even less.

● Allow time to relax. A non-stop round of theme-parking can be very exhausting, especially for small children. Noise levels within many attractions are high.

● If you leave any of the parks intending to return later in the day, get a hand-stamp of invisible ink at the turnstile.

● Do not prejudge either the parks or the attractions within them. Every one of Orlando's attractions is someone's favourite, and someone's least favourite. You cannot tell whether *you* will enjoy something unless you try it for yourself. The author's opinions of the rides and shows are simply that – the author's opinions.

● Health and safety warnings are posted all over the parks. They naturally err on the side of caution, but should not be ignored.

● Don't forget – you are here to enjoy yourself. Have a nice day!

THEME PARK TIPS

Theme Park Restrictions
In most parks, you are not allowed to do the following:
● Bring your own food or drink
● Enter without wearing a shirt, or without shoes
● Take flash photographs within most attractions
● Smoke in rides or shows, or while queueing for them
● Drink alcohol (specifically in Magic Kingdom)
● Use credit cards at fast-food restaurants (MasterCard, VISA and American Express are acceptable anywhere else).

Theme Park Facilities
Apart from these rules, the big parks are remarkably

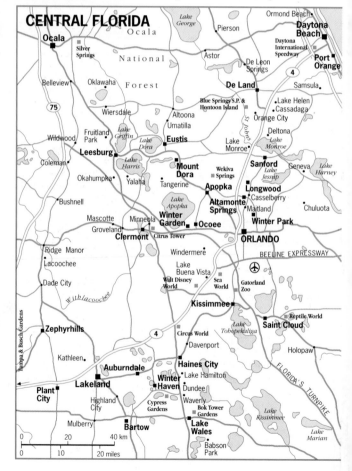

accommodating, making it easy for as many people as possible to use them. Among the many facilities available are: wheelchairs and strollers (pushchairs), rentable for a few dollars a day; baby-feeding and changing facilities (disposable nappies, or diapers, available in many shops); facilities for sight-or hearing-impaired visitors; handicapped parking places, staff assistance, and priority within attractions for wheelchair guests; lockers; an efficient lost and found system (including one for children); package pick-up systems for bulky purchases; help with special dietary requirements; kennels; first aid posts; banks; mail boxes and stamps; free transport from parking bays to ticket booths, and within or between parks; camera rental; plenty of clean, tidy WCs; public telephones; drinking fountains; information centres, and staff constantly on hand to help with any problems.

Sickness Ratings

Theme parks affect children differently. Many take the thrills completely in their stride; some get hooked on adrenalin and wildly excited; a few get frightened or sick.

None of the rides in any of the parks cause problems for the vast majority of users. Theme park staff do not want you throwing up all over the place, after all, and few rides last long enough for serious queasiness to develop.

However, listed on page 18 are a few things you might avoid if you or your children get nervous on thrill rides or are very susceptible to motion sickness. At any rate make sure the kids are not too full of jelly sandwiches before you start! If you are pregnant, or have a weak heart, back or neck, don't risk the joltier rides. If you are at all concerned, consult your doctor before you go.

Ponce Inlet

New Smyrna Beach

Edgewater

(95) Oak Hill

Canaveral

National

Seashore

Mims

Titusville

John F. Kennedy Space Center

Merritt Island N.W.R.

Spaceport USA-Visitors Center

Indian River

Cape Canaveral

Cape Canaveral

Cocoa

Merritt Island

Rockledge

Cocoa Beach

Satellite Beach

Indian Harbour Beach

Indialantic

Melbourne **Palm Bay**

Grant

(95)

Sebastian

Fellsmere

THEME PARK TIPS

Without question the wildest ride in any of Orlando's theme parks is the **Magic Kingdom Space Mountain**. The G-forces are hard on your spine and, because you are in the dark, you cannot predict or brace yourself for the movements. That is why the fans love it! More swoops and curves on the **Big Thunder Mountain Railroad** but, despite the screams, it is much less alarming than Space Mountain. **EPCOT Center Body Wars** is a simulated ride through the human body which some find disturbing as much for its subject matter as for any movement involved.

Disney–MGM Studios Star Tours is another simulated ride with dizzying visual effects, while **Universal Studios Back to the Future** is undoubtedly

Wet'n Wild theme park is based on an exciting swimming complex

the most 'intense' simulated experience here. The **Funtastic World of Hanna–Barbera** can be unsettling too.

Busch Gardens Python and **Scorpion** consist of classic old-fashioned roller-coasters where the ratchets creak in anticipation of downward plunges. Both execute 360-degree loops. The **Phoenix** and **Sandstorm** involve fairground-style swinging and whirling movements. Others to avoid if you are pregnant or have a weak heart are the **Congo River Ride**, the **Tanganyika Tidal Wave** and **Questor**. Some people find the **3-D CircleVision** shows (there are several in the EPCOT World Showcase pavilions) mildly disturbing. Nothing actually moves except the pictures on the curved screen, but the illusion of motion is very convincing, hence the rails for you to hold on to.

What to See

> Attractions are not always listed in strict alphabetical order under theme park names, but have been arranged by the author into the most useful sequences to best visit and enjoy each ride or show on the ground.

WALT DISNEY WORLD

This enormous resort complex covers some 43 square miles (111 sq km). Within it are three huge theme parks, two water parks, a nightclub theme park, almost 20 hotels (some of which are self-contained themed resorts), a massive campground, a villa complex, five golf-courses, numerous swimming pools and tennis courts, shops, restaurants, beaches, lakes, roads, woods, an impressive network of public transport, and dozens of individual attractions. As if this weren't enough, much, much more is planned over the next decade. Disney's Boardwalk, a 30-acre (12-ha) Coney Island-style amusement area, is due to open just west of the EPCOT Center in 1993. There are also plans for a possible fourth major theme park. Less than a quarter of the site has been developed: another quarter is designated a 'wilderness preserve'. Something over 80 million people have trudged 350 million times through those turnstiles since they first opened in 1971. On a busy day,

as many as 150,000 people may visit Walt Disney World.

Tickets (Passes)

Admission to the Disney parks goes like this:

● **Single-day tickets** are valid for one park only, (EPCOT Center, Magic Kingdom, or Disney–MGM Studios). All the major Disney parks charge the same admission, but prices change comparatively frequently.

● A **Four-day Passport** allows unlimited access to any of the three large parks, and free use of the transport systems between them (your four chosen days do not have to be consecutive and your passport lasts indefinitely).

● A **Five-day Super Pass** gives you five days' worth of all the features of a Four-day Passport, plus unlimited admission to WDW's other attractions – Typhoon Lagoon, Pleasure Island, Discovery Island and River Country, for one week after the first use of your pass. Certain combination tickets for the smaller attractions are also available; so are season passes, though these are unlikely to suit

WALT DISNEY WORLD

non-US holiday-makers.
Child passes are for ages 3–9;
younger ones enter free.

Which Pass to Choose?
Many package holidays to
central Florida include either a
four- or five-day pass to WDW.
Presumably if you are
considering this area as a
holiday destination you will
want to see Walt Disney World.
If you are spending just a week
here and plan to see some of
Florida's other attractions, it
may be better to take single-
day tickets to whichever Disney
theme parks interest you most.
You can, at a pinch, get a good
flavour of each of the big parks
in a day, though this will not
allow you time to linger in
shops or enjoy leisurely
lunches.
If you spend longer than a week
in Orlando, buy the Five-day
Super Pass: the water parks and
Pleasure Island are well worth
seeing, and provide a relaxing
antidote to the pressured
activity of the bigger parks.

Opening Hours
The major parks generally stay
open long hours, all day, every
day of the year. During periods
of exceptional crowding they
may close if they get full.
Precise opening times vary
according to seasonal demand,
and may change at short notice.
Check when you arrive in
Orlando at its Visitor
Information Center, or direct
with WDW (tel: 824 4321);
re-check whenever you arrive
at the parks. Gates usually open
at least half an hour before the
official opening time, and it is
well worth arriving as early as

you can to avoid queues and
make the most of your day.
Individual attractions close from
time to time for technical
reasons or for maintenance
(equipment safety is constantly
monitored), and some special
shows take place only when the
parks stay open late in the
evenings (usually the busiest
days, see below). Bad weather
rarely affects the large parks,
but may close water parks such
as the Typhoon Lagoon.

Avoiding the Crowds
Surprisingly, weekends (apart
from special holidays) are not
usually the most crowded
times. Busiest days at the Magic
Kingdom and EPCOT Center
are generally Monday to
Wednesday. Disney–MGM
Studios gets most traffic later in
the week, from Wednesday to
Friday. If the weather is bad, do
not cancel your visit; you will be
able to enjoy the parks in less
crowded conditions (in any
case, Florida weather rarely
stays gloomy for long). The
busiest holiday period is
between Christmas and New
Year. Thanksgiving weekend
and other US holidays, spring
break and Easter time are also
extremely busy. The parks are
quietest from Thanksgiving
weekend until the week before
Christmas.
EPCOT Center, the largest and
most challenging of the parks,
gives you the best introduction
to Walt Disney World, so visit
this first if you can. Then pass
on to the more light-hearted
Magic Kingdom, and the
somewhat more adult
Disney–MGM Studios last.

Travelling within WDW

The size of the Disney site makes it quite impractical to stroll about from park to park, so study a good map and bone up on how to get about. Road systems are very well signed, though they are complex and you will rapidly lose any sense of direction once within the World. Look out for landmarks (each park has one, visible for miles: Cinderella Castle, Spaceship Earth, the Earffel Tower), or hotels (the World Swan and World Dolphin are particularly striking). A car is not essential, but is definitely the most convenient way to get around Walt Disney World. Parking is free if you stay within WDW, otherwise it is about $4 at each theme park. Golden rule: remember where you leave the car! Disney transport is little short of miraculous, but

the sheer distances and crowds could delay your arrival time at the parks. Identification may be required on some routes (you are not entitled to use the transport between parks on single-day tickets, but staff sometimes turn a blind eye). Buses are all clearly flagged with different colours – pick up a plan which tells you which one to look out for. One circular loop of the monorail system links the resorts around the Seven Seas Lagoon in the Magic Kingdom with the Transportation and Ticket Center (TTC), and an inner loop travelling anticlockwise provides an express service. A second loop takes you southwards to EPCOT Center (change at TTC). Ferries ply across the lagoons, and through various canals to resort hotels and Disney–MGM Studios.

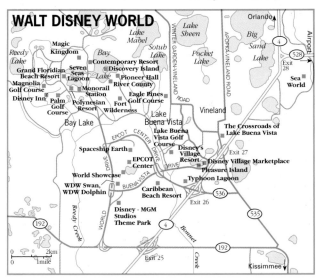

WALT DISNEY WORLD

EPCOT CENTER ✓

The second of WDW's great theme parks opened in October 1982, though Walt had already set the ball rolling shortly before his death in 1966. The name is a contraction of 'Experimental Prototype Community of Tomorrow', a cumbersome appellation that obscures more than it clarifies. The main concept behind this ambitious theme park is to provide a window on the world of new ideas and technologies. Walt Disney's original plans included an entire city with permanent residents and model industries.

EPCOT Center is more than twice the size of the Magic Kingdom, and more serious in tone, straying much further into the domain of education, though some would claim the educational content of EPCOT is fairly superficial. Many children under 10 will appreciate it only in part, and may be frankly bored by some of it. For all that, much of EPCOT is highly entertaining too, and the massive scale of its operations is nothing short of spectacular. Every part of the park is squeaky clean and beautifully (if sterilely) landscaped with neat gardens, obedient fountains and broad walkways, music pouring from loudspeakers at intervals.

EPCOT Center forms a rough figure-of-eight shape, and contains two separate elements: Future World and World Showcase. **Future World**, in the

Spectromagic with Mickey Mouse

The Living Seas exhibition

bottom ring of the '8', consists of a group of ten elaborate pavilions devoted to some aspect of modern life: agriculture and food production, communications, oceanology, health, energy, transport, and so on. Each pavilion houses a number of multimedia themed attractions. The focal landmark of EPCOT Center, visible for miles around, is a silvery geosphere like a massive golf-ball at the entrance to the park, known as **Spaceship Earth**. This unique futuristic structure is made of aluminium and weighs a million pounds (over 450 thousand kilos). When you get disorientated among EPCOT's bewildering range of attractions, just look for the silver ball.

The upper ring of the '8' is occupied by another of those artificial lakes so beloved by Disney landscapers. Around the edge of the lagoon lies the **World Showcase**, a group of pavilions depicting aspects of 11 (there are plans for two more) different countries. Collectively this attraction forms something not unlike a world trade fair, each nation promoting itself through its products, cuisine and tourist potential.

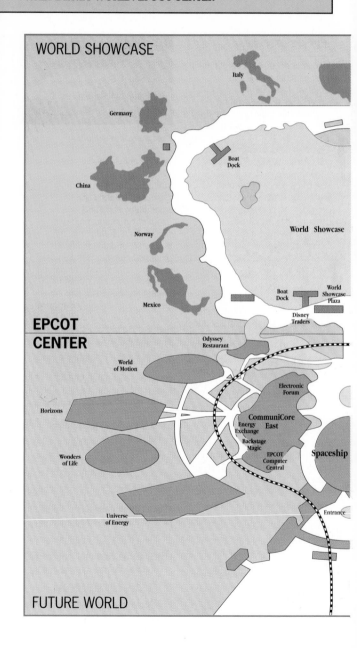

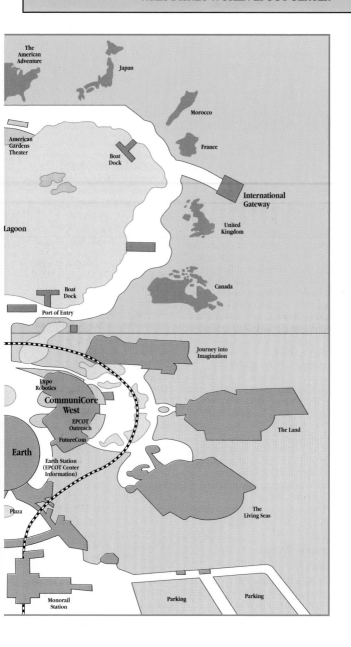

WALT DISNEY WORLD: EPCOT CENTER

Practical Details

To see absolutely everything at EPCOT you need longer than a day; however, it is unlikely you will be equally fascinated by all of it, and you can skim sections quickly if they do not interest you much. EPCOT's delights are envisaged as dynamic rather than static. New attractions and ideas are constantly being added, and obsolete ones withdrawn, so you may find things not as described below. You will be on your feet to explore Future World (unless someone is pushing a wheelchair or stroller for you), but you can traverse the World Showcase Lagoon by boat, or take a double-decker bus ride around the national pavilions. The same excellent guest facilities are available as in the other parks. All around EPCOT you will see WorldKey interactive video terminals offering touch-screen information and advice about the park facilities. You can even call up a real-live attendant to answer your questions on this two-way system ('How may I help you? Please don't be shy!'). One of the highlights of any EPCOT visit is the closing show called IllumiNations, a spectacular display of lasers, fireworks and coloured fountains when all the pavilions around the lagoon light up to music in turn.

Future World

♦♦
SPACESHIP EARTH

Inside the vast silver dome is a time-machine ride past animated tableaux depicting the achievements of humankind through the ages, from prehistoric cave dwellers to the space age. Queues can be very long. If so, try later in the day. At the base of the geosphere is **Earth Station**, EPCOT's main information and guest relations centre.

♦
COMMUNICORE WEST

A crescent-shaped pavilion housing FutureCom, an exhibition depicting multifarious methods of communication with video games and a 'fountain' of confusing information. Also in this section are **Expo Robotics** and **EPCOT Outreach**, a library information service with a teachers' center. Making much headway with these exhibits is time-consuming and quite hard work.

♦
COMMUNICORE EAST

Exhibits include **EPCOT Computer Central** (how computers rule our lives), **Energy Exchange** (video displays on fossil, solar, nuclear energy, and the like); **Electronic Forum** (live news broadcasts from around the world, and you are also invited to cast your vote for the 'Person of the Century' towards a new Disney attraction); **Travelport** ('vacation stations' give shatteringly superficial tourist information). Best in this pavilion is the **Backstage Magic** presentation where visitors get a peek at Disney's computer room and find out a bit about AudioAnimatronics, Disney's patent system of

animating those wonderfully lifelike models.

◆◆◆
THE LIVING SEAS

Most visitors find this pavilion extremely entertaining and well presented after the rather muddling experiences of CommuniCore. You descend in a marvellously futuristic diving ship to Sea Base Alpha, a fine aquarium exhibit with massive tanks and lots of tropical fish in a Florida reef setting. In the attractive and popular Coral Reef Restaurant you can gawp at fish, and eat them at the same time.

◆◆◆
THE LAND

An interesting pavilion devoted to food and agriculture (the emphasis on dairy products is not unconnected with its sponsorship by Kraft Foods). Needless to say, there is plenty to eat here, and it gets full of

On the Journey into Imagination

folk chomping chocolate cake around lunchtime. Other things to do include: **Listen to the Land**, a boatride through various inhospitable ecosystems, and a futuristic greenhouse using latest plant technology; **Kitchen Kabaret**, an amusing if slightly moralistic AudioAnimatronic show about nutrition; and **Harvest Theater**, showing a worthy film called *Symbiosis* about people and the environment.

◆◆
JOURNEY INTO IMAGINATION

Slightly disappointing. The so-so ride features Figment, a purple dragon, and Dreamfinder, a sort of Phileas Fogg adventurer piloting a flying machine in search of new ideas. **Captain EO**, a fantasy 3-D adventure featuring Michael Jackson, is a crazy stunt-filled rock and roll film. Warning: do not sit at the front for this – the effects do not work well at close range. **Image Works** involves lots of participatory stuff with electronic paintbrushes and an orchestra you conduct by waving your hands over a console. Greatest fun at this pavilion are the **Jumping Fountains** outside, which keep visitors goggling in amazement as disembodied, apparently solid arcs of water leap from one pool to another.

WORLD OF MOTION

It's Fun to be Free is an entertaining ride through the history of transport, from square wheels to space travel. The speedrooms are good. The **TransCenter** has walk-through displays on transport topics.

HORIZONS

Involves a single ride speculating on future developments such as robotic harvesters, holograph communication, underwater cities and zero-gravity living. At the end you can speed through a landscape of your choice. Worth catching.

WONDERS OF LIFE

A large pavilion housing several entertaining multimedia presentations relating to health and the human body. In the concourse you can measure your fitness on exercise machines and eat 'health' foods (chocolate milkshakes?). **Body Wars** is a jolty flight-simulated ride through the human body (see **Sickness Ratings**, page 17). **Cranium Command** is an excellent and very funny AudioAnimatronic show about the human brain. **The Making of Me** is pretty daring stuff for Disney – a film about sex (human reproduction, if you prefer). It is tastefully done and not at all embarrassing, engagingly presented by a boy speculating about where he came from. True to the Disney ethos, the participants fall in love and get married first.

UNIVERSE OF ENERGY

This extravagant presentation by the Exxon company is not to be missed. It is a truly remarkable ride in a huge

Sunshine reflected from the golden dome, the Wonders of Life pavilion

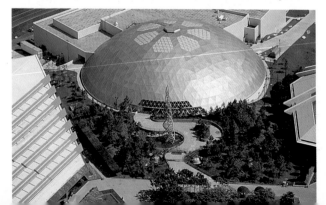

The China pavilion

travelling theatre. First you watch an animated film on fossil fuels (sharp intake of breath at shots of Port Valdise and Arctic pipelines). Then the seats split up and trundle off on an odyssey through a prehistoric forest with terrific dinosaurs and thunderstorms. It even smells of dank vegetation.

World Showcase

If you head here early in the day you will find the pavilions less crowded than in the afternoon. It does not matter whether you take them east–west, or the other way round. All the pavilions have some sort of appropriately themed architectural motif, one or more typical restaurant, shops selling national products, and sometimes live entertainment, film shows or other special attractions.
You can go behind the scenes on **Hidden Treasures of World Showcase**, a four-hour walking tour (over 16s only).

◆◆
CANADA
Totem poles and a Canadian landscape of rocky canyons

and waterfalls set the scene for *O Canada*, a CircleVision film about Mounties and other national glories. Le Cellier is a cafeteria-style restaurant.

◆
UNITED KINGDOM
The Rose and Crown pub is the centrepiece among what looks like a curious amalgam of Hyde Park, the Cotswolds and Edinburgh. You can buy Bass bitter here at about three dollars a half-pint. Shops sell Pringle woollies, Twinings tea, Royal Doulton china, and Crabtree & Evelyn cosmetics.

◆◆
FRANCE
Mansard roofs and a mini-Eiffel Tower pinpoint one of the best restaurants (*mais naturellement*) in the World Showcase, and lots of mouth-watering shops.
Impressions de France whirls visitors through undefined Gallic landscapes to French music. Camera effects are very impressive.

◆◆
MOROCCO
One of the most distinctive pavilions architecturally: a walled desert city with minarets and carved gateways. Belly-dancing goes on over couscous in the Marrakesh restaurant, and many traditional crafts are on display in the *medina*.

◆
JAPAN
Beautiful landscaping, the Bijutsu-kan Gallery, a Mitsukoshi Department Store, and several restaurants characterise this pagoda complex.

Mickey keeps an eye on his guests

◆◆◆
THE AMERICAN ADVENTURE
This takes centre stage, of course, involving an elaborately constructed replica of Philadelphia's Liberty Hall. The patriotic AudioAnimatronics show within is well worth seeing and lasts a stirring 29 minutes, with Ben Franklin and Mark Twain presiding over the historical production.

◆◆
ITALY
St Mark's Square sets the scene for Italian luxury goods and spaghetti, with live entertainment at the Teatro di Bologna.

◆◆
GERMANY
The main attraction is the Biergarten with traditional Germanic entertainment (oompah music) and folk-dancing in a setting of Grimm's Fairy Tale architecture. Souvenirs include lovely Hummel figurines.

◆◆◆
CHINA
A fine CircleVision film, *The Wonders of China*, is worth catching here. The restaurant is very pricey, but there are lots of souvenirs to buy.

◆◆
NORWAY
EPCOT's newest pavilion, featuring a thrill-ride through a fjord (**The Maelstrom**) as you come face to face with three-headed trolls and other creatures, plus lots of handicrafts and a restaurant.

◆◆◆
MEXICO
One of the most exciting pavilions visually, marked by pre-Columbian pyramids and exotic carvings. **El Rio del Tiempo** is an exciting boat ride through the ancient cultures of Central America, a fine if somewhat censored exhibition of art and a very pleasant restaurant, the San Angel.

THE MAGIC KINGDOM ✓

The Magic Kingdom is what most people think of when Walt Disney World is mentioned. This giant play-pen of fairies, monsters, and those immortal cartoon characters Mickey Mouse and friends, was the first section of WDW to be constructed, and is modelled closely on the original Disneyland theme park in California. Covering 100 acres (40 ha) with nearly 50 major attractions, it is on a larger scale than its Californian parent, and crowding is less intense. The focal point of the Magic Kingdom is **Cinderella Castle**, a Mad King Ludwig fantasy of spires and turrets visible from many parts of the park.

Practical Details

When you have parked and arrived at the ticket booths to the Magic Kingdom, you still have some way to go. To reach the attractions you must take either a monorail journey, or the ferry across the **Seven Seas Lagoon**. The ferry ride gives you the best view of Cinderella Castle, and allows child-like anticipation to build up nicely. Seen from a distance like a mirage across the Lagoon, the castle looks magical indeed. Up close it looks rather less exciting. However, it makes a useful landmark and rendezvous spot while you are in the park. The Magic Kingdom is divided into seven different 'lands' arranged round an island between **Main Street, USA** and Cinderella Castle known as the **Central Plaza**. These lands are

Main Street USA, Adventureland, Frontierland, Liberty Square, Fantasyland, Mickey's Starland and Tomorrowland. Most people naturally seem to tackle them clockwise from Main Street (the order in which they appear below), but if you duck and dive you may miss some of the queues. The main attractions are briefly outlined below, but throughout the park there are dozens of sideshows, shops and eating places to distract you, and what seems a continuous barrage of live entertainment: parades, stunts, marching bands, musicians and, of course, the cartoon characters wandering about ready to fascinate the kids – ('Hey look, there's Mickey!') – and to pose for endless photographs. Best of these diversions are the **Three o'clock Parade** (daily at 15.00hrs; best viewing point is Frontierland), and the wonderful night shows: **Spectromagic**, with over 30 dazzling floats, the firework show **Fantasy in the Sky**, and the **Floating Electrical Pageant** on Seven Seas Lagoon (visible from the Contemporary or Polynesian Resorts). These shows are extremely spectacular, but take place only when the park stays open late (peak season and some weekends). It is worth choosing a day when they happen for your visit to the Magic Kingdom. Check in advance. If your feet tire on your way through the Magic Kingdom, you can get round parts of the park on an old-fashioned steam train, or an aerial gondola.

Main Street USA

Once through the turnstiles this is the first section you encounter: a jolly stage-set of ornate shop fronts purporting to represent some idealised small-town American highstreet of yesteryear. They all house tempting shops, but try not to spend too long in these. Call at **City Hall** for any information you need on show times or meal reservations. You can take some short rides on horse-drawn buggies and old fire engines, and there are a few attractions to linger over in Main Street.

PENNY ARCADE

Vintage games machines and early animation viewers.

MAIN STREET CINEMA

Nostalgic Disney cartoons and old movies.

WALT DISNEY STORY

By far the most interesting thing in Main Street, though the worn soundtrack is quite difficult to hear and it may bore small children. Queueing is minimal. An avuncular Walt Disney recounts his life story from beyond the grave on tape and film, perhaps remembered just a little rosily in old age. It is a touching and affectionate portrait. As you wait to go into the theatre, look at the **Hall of Fame** where admiring letters from the great and famous (Churchill, U Thant) are proudly displayed amid some of Disney's many cinematic accolades.

Adventureland

Several excellent attractions here in varied tropical settings, all worth catching, and some appealing souvenirs and ice-creams.

SWISS FAMILY TREEHOUSE

A splendid den. Now is that banyan tree real, or not? It is not until you are high up in the leafy branches that the illusion cracks – only the dripping Spanish moss is genuine. Lots of steps to climb, and it can be a slow shuffle round the duckboards to see the homey rooms ('This is where we have our evening prayer', and so on).

JUNGLE CRUISE

An enjoyable if geographically faithless voyage through Amazon rainforests, the Nile valley, and a Southeast Asian jungle. Lots of animals on the way, and gas heaters concealed in the rocks to step up the temperatures.

PIRATES OF THE CARIBBEAN

A great adventure cruise with some of WDW's most sophisticated Audio-Animatronics technology. En route you pass elaborately constructed sets of wrecks, raids and castaways, some quite alarming for young children.

ENCHANTED TIKI BIRDS

A gentle, unfrenetic show where you can relax quietly in a

The night show Fantasy in the Sky is a special attraction

WALT DISNEY WORLD: THE MAGIC KINGDOM

thatched hut and enjoy hundreds of animated singing birds, flowers and tribal totems. Suitable for all ages.

Frontierland

Pioneer magic with an Old West flavour.

◆◆◆

BIG THUNDER MOUNTAIN RAILROAD

An exhilarating but not too terrifying roller-coaster ride through Arizona scenery and an old mining set where a mini-rockfall assails you. The journey is too fast to take in all the elaborate details of the ride, so it is one you could well do more than once. A new thrill-ride, **Splash Mountain**, will be open nearby in autumn 1992.

◆◆

TOM SAWYER ISLAND

A pleasant, though not wildly exciting, outdoor attraction reached by raft, based on Tom and Huck's adventures, with scary caves, mock forts and barrel bridges. Aunt Polly's Landing is a good place to relax with peanut butter and jelly sandwiches and watch the paddle-steamer cruise by.

◆◆

COUNTRY BEAR VACATION HOEDOWN

Corny but relentlessly engaging show with foot-stompin' animated bears and singing mooseheads. It is cleverly done and very raucous.

◆◆

DIAMOND HORSESHOE JAMBOREE

Enthusiastic, cheerful Western dance-hall show held several times a day. Note: reservations are usually needed, and you can book a place at the Diamond Horseshoe itself.

The Haunted Mansion

Liberty Square

Clapboard architecture and tidy gardens evoke an ambience of Yankee respectability and national pride. The **Liberty Tree**, a symbolic live oak recalling Boston Tea Party days, forms a focal point among the shops selling pricey 'antiques' and American heritage souvenirs. This is a pleasant place to relax on shady benches, have lunch at the Liberty Tree Tavern, or take a leisurely boat cruise in the heat of the day on the three-decker riverboat. Smaller **Mickey Fink Keel Boats** ply the same stretches of water. There are two very different attractions in this 'land'.

HALL OF PRESIDENTS

Cleverly done in its way, though it is hardly a barrel of laughs. Visitors get a basinful of the US Constitution, a rapid gallop through the Civil War, a flourish of the Stars and Stripes, and a reminder of the American Dream (lest we forget) from Abe Lincoln. The show includes a roll-call of US presidents, all carefully attired in correct period costume, and shuffling animatronically from time to time.

HAUNTED MANSION

Entertaining and mostly hilarious. Only the very susceptible will get any serious frights aboard this cobwebby ghost train and its 999 'happy haunts'. Transparent spectres whirl in a *danse macabre*, suits of armour clank into action, and a persistent raven hovers.

Fantasyland

In the shadow of the fairy-tale castle lies a collection of themed attractions ranging from the fictions of J M Barrie to Jules Verne. Older children may scorn simple fairground fun like **Dumbo the Flying Elephant**, the **Mad Tea Party** and **Cinderella's Golden Carousel**, but tinies love them. Fantasyland is understandably popular with the younger set and is consequently often crowded. Not all the rides repay the long waits.

IT'S A SMALL WORLD

Saccharine and schmaltzy, but the special effects are remarkable. It's a long boat ride through cavern after cavern of elaborately animated dolls, a medley of light and movement and infuriating tunes.

PETER PAN'S FLIGHT

Enjoyable, gentle journey through the sky suspended from an overhead rail.

20,000 LEAGUES UNDER THE SEA

Opinions differ widely on this one. It is an older ride, and the underwater illusions crack badly under pitiless comparisons with modern technology. Nevertheless, those monstrous green glass-bottomed 'submarines' into which you clamber are rather wonderful, and this attraction is very different from anything else at WDW. Try it if the queues are not too slow, but don't wait too long.

WALT DISNEY WORLD: THE MAGIC KINGDOM

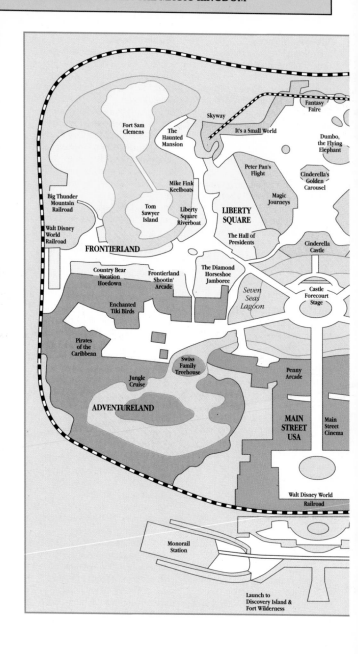

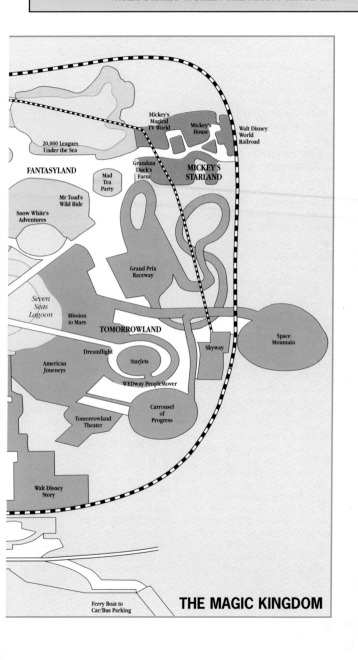

Mickey's
Magical
TV World

Mickey's
House

Walt Disney
World
Railroad

20,000 Leagues
Under the Sea

FANTASYLAND

Grandma
Duck's
Farm

MICKEY'S
STARLAND

Mad
Tea
Party

Mr Toad's
Wild Ride

Snow White's
Adventures

Grand Prix
Raceway

Seven
Seas
Lagoon

Mission
to Mars

TOMORROWLAND

Space
Mountain

Dreamflight

Skyway

American
Journeys

StarJets

WEDway PeopleMover

Tomorrowland
Theater

Carrousel
of
Progress

Walt Disney
Story

Ferry Boat to
Car/Bus Parking

THE MAGIC KINGDOM

WALT DISNEY WORLD: THE MAGIC KINGDOM

MAGIC JOURNEYS
A 3-D film-show, good in parts. Excellent high-tech camerawork gives remarkable special effects with the purple spectacles. The subject matter is exceedingly soft-focus.

SNOW WHITE'S ADVENTURES
The wicked queen tries to blight everyone's life. Unconvincing 2-D ghosts pop out at intervals, but there are some nice magic trees.

MR TOAD'S WILD RIDE
This attraction is perhaps the most disappointing of any in Walt Disney World, and it is high time it was scrapped or upgraded. See it only if there is a short wait.

Disneymania
If the kids tire of rides there is Disneymania – live singing and dancing shows with Mickey and the gang – which takes place in front of Cinderella Castle.

Mickey's Starland
This small section of the Magic Kingdom is something of an afterthought, and fits rather raggedly into the rest of the park. But this is the place to bring the kids if they really want to meet Mickey Mouse. In the afternoon there is a chance to meet more recent Disney characters, including 'Duck Tales' Scrooge McDuck and Launchpad McQuack. It also has a children's playground, and is a point to catch that nice little train from Main Street.

MICKEY'S MAGICAL TV WORLD
Live musical comedy featuring all those beloved Disney characters. After the show, meet them backstage in the dressing-room.

GRANDMA'S PETTING FARM
A dispiriting little complex of concrete pens and cages with a few chickens, calves, goats, and so on. Only for kids in danger of forgetting what real animals look like amid the Disney versions.

Tomorrowland
The cone-shaped pavilion housing Tomorrowland's star attraction vies with Cinderella's castle as a Magic Kingdom landmark. The rides in Tomorrowland vary in thrill-rating from heart-stopping to zero. Apart from missable amusement park stuff like StarJets and the Grand Prix Raceway (dodgems without the dodging), many attractions have the worthy educative stamp of EPCOT Center. Several are sponsored by big corporations, and there is a distinct feeling of being clobbered by marketing men in this section of the park.

SPACE MOUNTAIN
For many visitors, this is the favourite attraction of the Magic Kingdom, if not the whole of WDW. Addicts can spend all day just doing this ride. Unless you are pregnant, have a medical problem, or hate roller-coaster rides, you just

WALT DISNEY WORLD: THE MAGIC KINGDOM

have to do this one. If you have done roller-coasting before, then Space Mountain will present few terrors. But the special effects and the adrenalin build-up as you queue make this a pretty wild two-and-a-half minutes by any standards. No children under 3; children under 7 should be accompanied by adults (though quite often it seems like the other way round!).

The Space Mountain building covers a 10-acre (4-ha) site and rises 180 feet (55m) above the Magic Kingdom. Within its

Space Mountain

45,000,000 cubic feet (about 125 cubic metres) a roller-coaster snakes through the darkness on mammoth beams of pre-stressed concrete. The ride is computer controlled from a weird blue glow of dials and monitors, which prospective passengers see as they wait. The angst-factor is heightened by warning notices, and the fact that the slow-moving queues cannot see what is going on up there. You only hear the screams!

Gradually you reach the point of no return. This is your last chance to leave the line. Non-quitters are strapped firmly into their cars, three or four at a time. Anchor down all loose objects, including your breakfast. If you are feeling timid, do not ride in the front seat (there is always some nutcase who actually *likes* doing that). Then you are off, hurtling through the strobe-lights. It feels supersonic as the G-forces rack your spine and leave your stomach somewhere in orbit. Nervous passengers will be relieved to hear that infra-red cameras monitor this ride at all stages.

◆◆
CAROUSEL OF PROGRESS

After the thrills of Space Mountain, this gentler attraction may wind you down. It is a hammy, sentimental show with an embarrassing song in best Disney tradition, but for all that it is disarmingly warm and nostalgic, with touching optimism in future progress. Animated tableaux depict the way in which electricity has made all our lives (particularly those of Mr and Mrs Middle America and their dog) a whole lot happier.

◆
DREAMFLIGHT

A Delta Airlines production about the history of flight, good in parts but insufficiently sustained.

◆
WEDWAY PEOPLEMOVER

This ponderous ride in a linear induction-powered mass transportation system (any the wiser?) gives you a chance to decide you do not like the look of Space Mountain, but not much else. Environmentally, though, it is all edifying stuff.

AMERICAN JOURNEYS

All-embracing travelogue projected on a 360-degree screen, featuring good-tempered hoedowns round the ole' camp fire and other mythical aspects of modern America, against a background of luscious scenery and evocative muzak.

Restaurants

Pick up snacks or fast food as you go round: for example, at the **Columbia Harbour House** in Liberty Square (imaginative sandwiches, salads), **Adventureland Verandah** (chicken teriyaki) and the **Mile Long Bar**, Frontierland (Mexican specialities). The **Lunching Pad** in Tomorrowland serves fresh fruit, yoghurt and natural juices. The nicest places for a sit-down meal are **Tony's Town Square Restaurant** (mostly Italian) and the **Liberty Tree Tavern** (reservations accepted), where you can enjoy a decent seafood chowder. You get a cold sandwich platter if you have booked the lunchtime **Diamond Horseshoe Jamboree** show. The **Crystal Palace** at the far end of Main Street is a pleasant and generally uncrowded cafeteria. Dining at **King Stefan's Banquet Hall** in the Cinderella Castle can be particularly disappointing and crowded.

DISNEY–MGM STUDIOS ✓

Opened in 1989, this is (to date) the latest of Disney's big theme parks. It provides a showcase for the huge range of Disney TV and film productions, which now cater for adults as well as children. The Walt Disney Company has obtained rights to use the weighty name and productions of Metro–Goldwyn–Mayer to illuminate more than half a century of motion-picture making. Orlando now has a great rival film-world attraction in the shape of Universal Studios. Both are enjoyable and well worth seeing, but it is better to see the Disney version first. Disney-MGM Studios re-creates the aura of heyday Hollywood from the 1930s onwards, as those of us who were never there like to imagine it. Against a backdrop of Art Deco sets and yesteryear automobiles, visitors find many of today's screen celebrities brought to life with the latest technology and dramatic special effects, from Muppets to Indiana Jones. Needless to say, Mickey Mouse is remembered too, most noticeably in Disney–MGM's most striking landmark, the Earffel Tower (a water tower near the main entrance crowned with those unmistakable round black ears).

Practical Details

The immense popularity of Disney–MGM Studios took Disney planners by surprise, and since the park first opened

Encounters on the Great Movie Ride

The Earffel Tower at dusk

get around mostly on foot, though the backstage tour includes a tram ride. Several attractions, however, involve lengthy sit-downs for films and shows, so there are plenty of chances to rest your feet in the shade. Shops, restaurants, and all the usual Disney facilities for visitors can be found at the Studios. Among the usual mass-produced range of Disneyana clutter and Mouse Ears, you can find more genuine reminders of why Walt Disney is a household name, such as original animation 'cels' – drawings for the early cartoons.

In addition to the main attractions and regular shows that go on all day, look out for constant music and entertainment in the 'streets'. Spot the daily celebrity who appears in the SuperStar TV show and leads a parade of vintage vehicles down **Hollywood Boulevard** at about 14.00hrs. When the park stays open late, a fireworks and laser show called **Sorcery in the Sky** takes place at the end of the day. Disney characters appear with singers and dancers in musical cabaret shows in the **Theater of the Stars**. Pick up a schedule of special events from the **Production Information Window** as you enter the park.

◆

HOLLYWOOD BOULEVARD
This palm-lined street leading directly ahead from the main turnstiles takes you straight into old Tinseltown as it never really was. On either side lie neon-chrome Art Deco shopfronts selling Hollywood memorabilia and collectibles of one sort or

it has expanded greatly, with many plans afoot for further attractions. Currently it is around the size of the Magic Kingdom, but is still very much a working TV and film studio; large parts of it are off-limits or accessible only by guided tour. Crowding can be a problem at times. As in the other parks, it is advisable to arrive early (particularly for **Star Tours** and the **Magic of Disney Animation**) and use plenty of initiative to queue creatively! The Studios' attractions can, however, be comfortably seen within a single day.

It is the most southerly of the theme parks, well signed from the Maingate entrance. There is parking for 4,500 vehicles, with tram transport to the ticket booths, and lots of buses ply regularly to other parts of WDW. You can also reach Disney–MGM Studios by boat from the EPCOT Center resort hotels (World Swan, World Dolphin, Yacht and Beach Club Resorts). Within the park you another. As you wander past the classic cars littering the street you will probably encounter a bustle of autograph hunters, news reporters, film crews, talent spotters and hopeful starlets (all part of Team Disney, of course). Extrovert visitors may be dragged into a spot of limelight for a brief glimmer of stardom. You can even engineer a little fame at **Cover Story**, and have your photo glamorously splashed on a magazine. Or immortalise yourself on home video at **Pacific Electric Pictures** or **Sights and Sounds**.

◆◆◆
THE GREAT MOVIE RIDE

At the top of Hollywood Boulevard is a full-sized replica of Hollywood's famous **Chinese Theater**, which houses the Studios' first major attraction. It is popular, and you may have quite a wait, but make sure you see it at some stage during your visit. This elaborate multimedia ride through sound-stage sets from many classic Hollywood greats is a real *tour de force*, and one of the biggest and most ambitious attractions within WDW. On your tram ride you will encounter over a hundred extraordinarily realistic models, including James Cagney, John Wayne, Gene Kelly, Julie Andrews and Harrison Ford. To add spice to the adventure, your train will be ambushed by bank robbers and threatened by a hideous Alien before passing into the more romantic climes of *Casablanca* and *The Wizard of Oz*.

◆◆◆
BACKSTAGE STUDIO TOUR

Again, not to be missed. This section of Disney–MGM Studios, incidentally, is far more successful than the rival version at Universal Studios. Highlights of the long but fast-paced and always entertaining tram tour include **Catastrophe Canyon**, where an impressive earthquake and a flash flood are staged for your delight. (Protect your camera if you sit on the left.) You get to see literally 'behind the scenes' of those realistic-looking Hollywood villas used for suburban shots (they are mere shells at the back), inspect the costume, lighting and props departments, and discover how those elaborately painted trick-perspective Manhattan flats can be readily adapted for Anytown USA. Second stage of the tour is on foot through **Roger Rabbit's Looney Bin** shop to a special effects tank where you can see how a naval battle and a storm at sea can be filmed in a duckpond, and a hapless audience participant gets drenched. Towards the end of the tour you watch a short film recounting Bette Middler's crazy adventures with a winning lottery ticket. This pacy little number was entirely produced at the Studios; the convincing special effects are fully explained.

The **Post-Production** section investigates the mysteries of sound, computer effects and editing, and is worth seeing. To catch everything working, this tour is best taken after 13.00hrs.

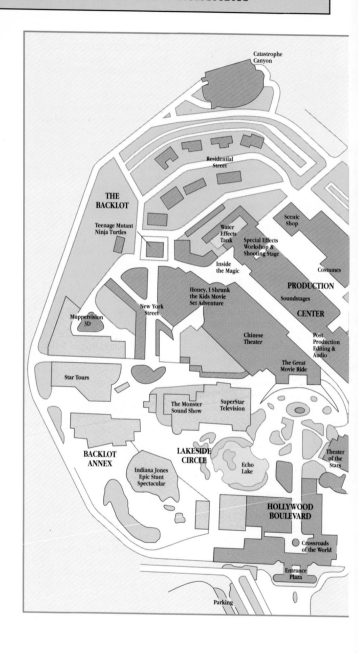

DISNEY–MGM STUDIOS THEME PARK

Earffel Tower

BACKSTAGE STUDIO TOUR

Walt Disney Theater

Backstage Shuttle Station

The Magic of Disney Animation

◆◆
SUPERSTAR TELEVISION

Young hopefuls are chosen to star in the show, egged on by enthusiastic comperes. Successful volunteers get to work on a chocolate-packing line with Lucille Ball, or take a lead in a scene from *General Hospital*.

◆◆◆
THE MAGIC OF DISNEY ANIMATION

This is splendid, featuring an unlikely but hilarious combination of Robin Williams and Walter Cronkite in a film about the basic techniques of animation. Afterwards, visitors troop through the animation studios to peer over the shoulders of Disney's huge team of artists, working through storyboards and rough pencil sketches to painstakingly coloured finished artwork. Computers help these days, but a surprising amount of cartoon work still involves the time-honoured hand-drawn method of figures replicated thousands of times on individual 'cels'. How much of the technology you absorb in one circuit is up to you, but you can always have another shot at it if you like.

At work in the animation studios

MONSTER SOUND SHOW

This is a theatre show involving a lot of fun with sound effects. Lots of Gothic mock-horror and audience participation. If you get hooked on this type of thing, you can play about with it in **Soundworks** at the end of the show, a series of participatory activities with sound equipment – you can even dub your voice into a famous scene.

INDIANA JONES EPIC STUNT SPECTACULAR

A popular and, as the title suggests, exciting show demonstrating professional stunts (some of them highly dangerous) in an adventure movie. Members of the audience volunteer as extras and come in for a fair amount of ridicule, but it is very enjoyable and very watchable. It is also one of the few shows in WDW where you are allowed to take photographs or use camcorders.

STAR TOURS

This space simulation flight includes some of WDW's most amazing visual special effects. If they get too intense, you can always shut your eyes. You should not miss it, but take the health warnings seriously. The crash landing through New York's skyscrapers is definitely not for plane phobics. The techniques and sensations are very similar to those used in the attraction called Body Wars at EPCOT Center. If you can cope with one, you will probably be all right on the other.

MUPPETVISION 3-D

Even if the Muppets are not on your favourite TV-character list, this musical show is highly entertaining and may well win you over. Since Muppet creator Jim Henson's untimely death, the precise terms of Disney's contract with the Muppets have been the subject of an acrimonious dispute, and how much longer the Muppets will grace WDW is anyone's guess. But if they are still there, make sure you see the show.

HONEY I SHRUNK THE KIDS MOVIE SET ADVENTURE

Young children may find this walk-through adventure playground with everything scaled up to Brobdignagian proportions entertaining, but for many people this attraction is one of the weaker and less convincing sections of Disney–MGM Studios.

Restaurants

As usual in Disney parks, there are plenty of places for quick snacks. Disney–MGM Studios, however, is the one park where (if you plan to spend all day) you can probably fit in a reasonably leisurely lunch and still see most things. Best choice for a sit-down meal is the faithfully reproduced **Hollywood Brown Derby** restaurant on Hollywood Boulevard. Make a reservation early in the day and try to hit it off-peak. The setting is elegant and classy in teak, mahogany and brass; the food pretty good by theme park standards (cobb salad and grapefruit cake are

house specialities). Other popular choices include the '50s **Prime Time Café's Tune In Lounge**, evoking a Fifties kitchen atmosphere of plastic laminate tables and pull-down lamps, with television screens everywhere you look. The food is typical of the era (copious and unremarkable), but the waitresses play Mom cheerfully, and as you eat you can watch lots of vintage

The amazing special effects of Star Tours are not for the faint-hearted!

sitcoms on video monitors (reservations recommended). For a simpler snack in a carefully designed 'set', try the **Backlot Express** – 600-seat counter service amid the props and paint-splashed floors of a working studio, with charbroiled chicken, salsa, burgers and chili.

OTHER ATTRACTIONS IN WALT DISNEY WORLD

After you have exhausted the possibilities of the three big theme parks of the Magic Kingdom, EPCOT Center, and Disney–MGM Studios, there is still plenty else to detain you at Walt Disney World. If you have a Five-day Super Pass you can visit any of these smaller attractions (Pleasure Island, Typhoon Lagoon, River Country and Discovery Island) as often as you like within five days of first using your pass for the big parks. Separate admission charges for all of them currently add up to around $50 for an adult; Disney Village is free.

Water-chutes in River Country sweep down into Bay Lake

DISCOVERY ISLAND
A small attraction covering just over 11 acres (4.5 ha) in **Bay Lake**, reached by regular shuttle boats from various points, including the Magic Kingdom resort hotels. You can easily combine a visit there with a trip to River Country or Fort Wilderness. There is not a great deal to do beyond wander round the boardwalks through exotic vegetation and look at exotic animals and birds, but it is a peaceful place to take a picnic (there is only a small snack bar on the island itself). Bird shows are held at intervals.

DISNEY VILLAGE MARKETPLACE
Everyone visiting Walt Disney

World runs across this complex around the **Buena Vista Lagoon** at some point. The Village consists of the official 'Plaza' hotels, shops, and eating places (many described in other sections). There is no entrance charge, and always something going on, including masses of boats to hire. Special events often take place, celebrities visit to be lionised, and the **Marketplace** shops are an entertainment even if you do not buy anything. Most of the Village is dedicated to pure entertainment, but the **Crossroads Shopping Center** is the place for practical matters, including a bank, post office, pharmacy and supermarket.

PLEASURE ISLAND

Pleasure Island offers a package of shops, restaurants and nightlife similar to Church Street Station (see page 63), but it has a completely different atmosphere. If you are keen on nightlife, see both. If you have to choose just one, Church Street has the edge in terms of decorative interest and the sustained quality of its shows. The Disney version occupies a six-acre (2.4-ha) site on a man-made island, linked to the Village Marketplace by several bridges. Pleasure Island's 'theme' is based on a fanciful tale about a 19th-century adventurer who bequeathed a chandlery and sailmaking business to his wastrel sons. The sets are vaguely reminiscent of sail-lofts and warehouses, albeit with a

spanking new, squeaky clean and synthetic Disney touch. Pleasure Island is essentially a nightlife attraction (with a 'New Year's Eve party' every night), but some shops and restaurants stay open all day and you can visit the island free until 19.00hrs. After this an admission fee which is currently over $12 per adult is charged. For this you get unlimited access to any of its ten cinema studios or half-dozen nightclubs (shows last 20–30 minutes and are frequently staged, so you can catch all of them in an evening). The action hots up quickly with neon and noise as soon as the park opens, and it is a place where children, teenagers and older people can mix happily (under-18s must be accompanied by an adult, and there are age restrictions on one or two attractions). All the nightclubs at Pleasure Island serve alcohol, but Florida drink laws are strict and anyone looking youthful enough to be under 21 must have identification.

Open: till 02.00hrs (some shops and attractions close earlier). Shows include a mix of bizarre comedy at the **Comedy Warehouse**, and **Adventurers' Club**, a two-storey building stuffed with colonial paraphernalia of animal heads and tribal totems (the sets are more entertaining than the shows); loud rock and dance music at **CAGE**, **Mannequins Dance Palace**, and **XZFR Rock and Roll Beach Club**; live country and western music at **Neon Armadillo Music Saloon**, and lots of subsidiary attractions – eye-catching shops selling zany novelties, and touts offering to guess your age, weight or date of birth. For eating, older folks head for the stately elegance of the Mississippi stern-wheeler, *Empress Lilly*, permanently anchored next to Pleasure Island, whose brightly lit decks contain several dressy and fairly pricey restaurants. The younger set may prefer the casual chic of **Fireworks Factory** (dynamite barbecues and explosive drinks), or faster food at **Maxwell's Diner**.

RIVER COUNTRY

This water park in a corner of **Fort Wilderness** conjures up an archetypal American dream: Huck Finn's perfect swimming hole, a place of prelapsarian innocence in completely (well, almost) natural surroundings. In fact, River Country is a painstaking piece of engineering, with rocky mountain landscapes scarcely native to central Florida, rope swings and flume rides, chutes, pools, fountains and rapids, all plunging round one of the biggest swimming pools hereabouts, a carefully filtered and walled-off section of **Bay Lake**. Quieter types may prefer the white-sand beaches and nature walks through cypress swamps, or just messing about in any of a dozen types of watercraft for hire on the lake. Bass fishing trips can be arranged.
Open: 10.00–17.00hrs, with extended hours in summer and

holidays (admission can be combined with Discovery Island).

TYPHOON LAGOON

The largest and most beautiful water park in Orlando, a lovely place to unwind if all those rides are getting a bit much. The wrecked shrimp boat precariously perched on a man-made mountain, and the windswept rakishness of the park buildings suggest a turbulent time. You can have exciting adventures here among the water-slides and rapids and exotic fish, but if you just want to relax and curl up in a hammock amid luxuriant tropical gardens, this is the spot. The well-tended park covers 56 acres (23 ha), its prize central feature a splendid surf lagoon with four-foot (1.2m) waves (which calm down at intervals). Lifeguards are on duty in all the watery places. Try the **Shark Reef** and snorkel with harmless versions of Jaws, or whirl gently through a rain forest in an inflatable dinghy on **Castaway Creek**, a continuous 'river' which provides the only form of transport around the Lagoon. For refreshments, graze on fast food and salad at **Leaning Palms** or **Typhoon Tilly's Galley and Grog**. You are allowed to bring your own food into the Typhoon Lagoon (but no alcohol), and there are shady picnic areas.
Open: daily 10.00–17.00hrs, with extended hours in season. Note: in bad weather the Typhoon Lagoon may be closed.

On the Typhoon Lagoon

OTHER MAJOR THEME PARKS

SEA WORLD ✓

You cannot spend any time at all in Orlando before realising that Mickey Mouse has a great rival for the affections of sentimental animal-lovers. Worse news for Mickey, this animal is real. Sea World's improbable star exhibit is a killer whale called Shamu. Although several killer whales have been born at Sea World, when Shamu gave birth in 1989 her adoring public fell into raptures. Film footage of the last few minutes of this extraordinary labour are endlessly recycled on video screens throughout the theme park. Shamu makes several graceful pirouettes, then torpedoes her 7-foot (2.1m) long baby half-way across the enormous aquarium. After two seconds of surprise at this abrupt entry into the world (can

killer whales blink?), Baby Namu is swimming perfectly, effortlessly, next to momma. Lovely stuff for the marketing men! Shamu's distinctive black and white shape is now Sea World's emblem, logo, and principal crowd-puller.

Sea World is one of the Busch Entertainment Corporation's theme parks, owned by Anheuser–Busch, the brewers who bring you Budweiser and Michelob (there is a working brewery on site). It is undoubtedly one of Orlando's major attractions, and most people seem to love it, whatever their reservations about keeping large sea mammals in captivity. It is obviously a sensitive issue, as indicated by Sea World's painstaking, backward-bending attempts to emphasise to all comers their sincere commitment to conservation, education, and research. Certainly the conditions in which Sea World's exhibits are housed seem very comfortable, however cramping a mere five million gallons (over 22 million litres) of man-made sea water must seem after the freedom of the ocean.

Anthropomorphists untroubled by any understanding of animal conditioning may assert that a bored or discontented Shamu would simply yawn and swallow at a gulp the daring trainers who romp with her. But how happy Shamu really is must remain a mystery, for unlike sharks, whose fearful teeth are clamped permanently in an attitude of moronic viciousness, the jaws of whales seem to form benevolent, intelligent smiles. How comforting for us!

Practical Details

Sea World is well signposted and easy to find, near the intersection of Highway I-4 and the Beeline Expressway (Exit 27A). There is a large free parking lot. You can see everything comfortably within a day at Sea World, including stops for meals. Though Sea World is apparently one of the largest marine parks in the world, it is nowhere near as extensive in area as the Disney theme parks. Still, it is advisable to arrive when the gates open, and plan your morning exploration around the show times. These are sensibly scheduled so that, if you move fairly sharply between one and the next, you can see all the attractions quite efficiently. It is a good plan to head swiftly to the far side of the park (**Terrors of the Deep**) when you first arrive and leave the crowds floundering about near the entrance.

The Shamu shows are very popular, so turn up early to get a good seat. (A 'good' seat at a Shamu show, incidentally, depends on your love of water. The first 14 rows get soaked by a playful killer whale dusting up a mini-tidal wave. Watch your camera!)

Sea World has similar facilities to WDW for visitors: stroller and wheelchair rental, nappy-changing areas, first aid posts, currency exchange, rentable

lockers, kennels, and so on, and everything is similarly well kept, clean, and attractive, though landscaping lacks the Disney sparkle. Smoking is not permitted within the attraction areas. Staff are pleasant and friendly, the tone set by the sign saying 'Thank you for visiting us. Making friends is our business.'

Open: year-round 09.00–20.00hrs (08.30–21.00hrs in summer and at holiday times). Some of the main attractions are listed below, but new shows are being planned all the time – **Mission: Bermuda Triangle** (a ride simulator) and **Shamu's Happy Harbor** (for children) opened in 1992, for example, as did the Anheuser–Busch Hospitality Center.

TERRORS OF THE DEEP

A relatively new attraction at Sea World, this otherwise interesting exhibit suffers from an excess of hype. Accompanied by menacing music at the entrance you pass two pools of manageably small sharks flapping about like goldfish, then proceed into a dark tunnel flanked by frilly lionfish in Barbara Cartland-style ballgowns, and the weird puffer fish which can blow themselves up like balloons. Barracuda attacks on humans, say the child-like handwritten notices, are quite rare and accidental – usually a case of mistaken identity. Well, that *is* nice to know.

Next comes a video show about sharks, comforting us with the fact that twice as many people die from bee-stings each year as from shark attacks, and that, in any case, sharks are not specifically designed to eat humans. They merely act as the ocean's garbage disposal unit. The screen rolls up to reveal a giant tank of real sharks, through which visitors next proceed, via a tunnel made of high-tech 6-inch-thick (15cm) plastic tubing capable of withstanding the weight of three elephants per square foot (900 sq cm). Somehow these sharks look rather tame and small, despite their ferocious reputation – it is not quite the Jaws experience the publicity leads you to expect.

◆◆◆
PENGUIN ENCOUNTER
This is delightful. Several species of these comical

creatures live in apparent harmony in what seems to be a fair attempt at a natural habitat. Snow and ice fall from the skylights, and mini-glaciers tumble down the rocks. Through their glazed enclosure you can see the penguins moving both on land and below the waterline, when they look quainter than any Disney animation. The second half of this attraction displays the Arctic cousins of the penguins: puffins and auks. If anything, these are even more appealing, scudding about like small robots.

◆◆
SEA LION AND OTTER SHOW
A silly but quite funny and even mildly educative show featuring

Attractions here are definitely live

SEA WORLD

waddling sea lions, a cheeky otter, and a splendidly hideous walrus. It is slapstick stuff with Mr Mean, the prehistoric litterbug, determined to mess up his environment.

WHALE AND DOLPHIN STADIUM

This show involves the kind of circus tricks animal rights activists protest about. Beluga whales, bottlenose dolphins and killer whales jump and pirouette with wet-suited trainers on their noses. Their tanks look relentlessly concrete, and the music is enough to hurt anyone's ears, let alone a sensitive dolphin's.

SHAMU STADIUM

The mega-star and her relatives cavort in an enormous stadium, where a vast video screen makes life easier for those at the back. The audience also has the fun of seeing itself get wet as Shamu tips half her tank on the front rows. Some lucky little person gets to sit on Shamu's back.

SEA WORLD THEATER

A slightly pedestrian presentation called *Windows to the Sea*, showing the value of marine conservation and stressing Sea World's part in it. Shamu gives birth yet again on video.

WATERSKI SHOW

A couple of shows a day are held in the Atlantis Waterski Stadium, with stunt skiing and waterski ballet.

Between Shows

Between the main shows, you can wander round petting stingrays (harmless, apparently, but definitely not cuddly), or the more terrestrial and appealing Anheuser–Busch Clydesdale horses. There's a 400-foot (122m) Sky Tower to climb (small additional entrance charge), aviaries, rockpools, playgrounds, and harbour seals waiting for you to throw them a fish. If you are seriously interested in the work of Sea World, book yourself on a 90-minute **Behind-the-Scenes** tour and find out about breeding, research and training programmes. In the evenings there is a grand finale called **Night Magic**, with lasers and fireworks. From just after 18.30hrs until after the park officially closes, you can enjoy a Polynesian Luau dinner show with hula dancers and fire jugglers.

Restaurants

Apart from the Polynesian dinner, food experiences at Sea World are mostly of the 'grazing' variety, that is, fast food to keep you going rather than stuff of any deep gastronomic significance. Choose from **Mama Rosa's Italian Kitchen**, **Hot Dogs and Spuds**, **Chicken 'n Biscuit**, the **Waterfront Sandwich Grill**, the **Dockside Grill** (smoked chicken and rib) or the **Spinnaker** (hamburgers). For a quick, inexpensive filler, try one of Pancho's Tacos or a Mexican 'Burrito' (a pancake-like roll of mince, cheese and beans), near the Stingray Lagoon.

UNIVERSAL STUDIOS ✓

This star-studded production of 'Hollywood goes to Florida' is the latest thing to hit Orlando. A massive new theme park of 444 acres (180 ha), Universal Studios was some four times the size of WDW's comparable attraction, the Disney–MGM Studios, when it first opened in June 1990 (since then the Disney park has expanded). The Disney Company saw the competition looming way back in the early 1980s, and rushed ahead with plans for its own movie theme park, pipping Universal Studios to the post by opening early in 1989. Now you can see, and compare, both.

Disney–MGM or Universal?
Since virtually every Orlando visitor goes to Walt Disney World (the main reason for taking a holiday in central Florida), the choice is not so much *which* film park to see, as whether to visit *both*. Most tourists will have the chance to see the Disney version on an inclusive pass. If so, visit Disney–MGM Studios first, and if you find it enjoyable and interesting, go and see Universal's blockbuster on a much larger scale. The two

UNIVERSAL STUDIOS

1. Alfred Hitchcock: The Art of Making Movies	10. Gory, Gruesome & Grotesque Horror Make-up Show	19. New York Street Sets
2. An American Tail Theater	11. Hard Rock Cafe	20. Nickelodeon Studios
3. Animal Actors Stage	12. Hollywood Boulevard	21. Production Studio Tour
4. Amity and Jaws	13. International Food Bazaar	22. San Francisco/ Fisherman's Wharf
5. Back to the Future.... The Ride	14. Kongfrontation	23. Screen Test Home Video Adventure
6. Café La Bamba	15. Louie's Italian Restaurant	24. Studio Stars Restaurant
7. E. T. Adventure	16. Mel's Drive-In	25. The Funtastic World of Hanna-Barbera
8. Earthquake–The Big One	17. Murder She Wrote! Mystery Theater	26. Wild, Wild, Wild West Stunt Show
9. Ghostbusters	18. New England	27. World Expo

UNIVERSAL STUDIOS

parks are quite different in flavour, and the material within them does not essentially overlap. If you liked one, you are not likely to be bored by the other. Both are absolutely worth seeing, box office hits by two giants of the entertainment industry – a great day out for anyone even faintly swayed by the glamour of celluloid. Universal Studios is a joint venture owned by MCA Inc (a hugely diversified leisure and entertainment conglomerate now in Japanese hands) and the British-based Rank Organisation plc. The complex cost around $630 million to build, and as well as a theme park it is a busy working film and TV production studio, the largest outside Hollywood. Billed as the 'ultimate interactive experience', it is a chance to ride the movies, and watch a dream factory in action.

Practical Details

Just as Walt Disney World is a spin-off from its Californian parent, Disneyland, Universal Studios Florida is closely

Take in the thrills – and spills – of the Earthquake ride

modelled on the original theme park in Hollywood. Many of the rides and ideas are similar, though the method of visiting them differs. In Hollywood you see all the attractions in one continuous tram tour, carefully scheduled to a smooth operation that avoids any queueing. In Florida all the attractions are separate, as in the Disney theme parks. You can pick and choose, and see them in any order, but you have to wait in interminable lines for each one. It involves the visitor in far more mental effort.

To see all the attractions at Universal Studios Florida you need every bit of a long day, especially if it is busy. You have to plan which things to see first, organise yourself to catch the shows at specific times, and constantly try to outwit the queues. Seeing the shows logically, in a way that will illuminate the process of film-making, is therefore unlikely. The sheer scale of the park is initially bewildering, and many of the shows seem to start simultaneously, so if you just miss the start of one it can be frustratingly difficult to find an alternative. Getting to see everything in a single day can be fairly stressful. On the other hand, there is not really enough to make it worth coming back for a second day unless you want to do some of the rides or shows more than once (two-day tickets are available for real movie buffs).

It is important, then, to arrive early at Universal Studios, at least half an hour before the official opening time (09.00hrs). Parking costs about the same as at the big Disney parks. All the facilities and house rules are similar to those at Walt Disney World: strollers, wheelchairs, guest relations, lockers, banking, camera rental, and so on, are all provided in the Front Lot near the main entrance. There are height restrictions and health requirements for some of the rides (no pregnant ladies in the Earthquake!). Children under 2 are admitted free, and there is reduced admission for under-10s. Universal Studios is a fairly adult attraction, and it is unlikely that very small children will get a great deal out of it. Some of the experiences are (as they say in Orlando) 'intense' and could be disturbing to sensitive youngsters.

Getting There
Universal Studios is located between Walt Disney World and downtown Orlando, where Highway I-4 meets Florida's Turnpike road. There are two car entrances to the theme park side of Universal Studios. Take Exit 30B from I-4 on to Kirkman, or Exit 29 to Sand Lake, then Turkey Lake. It is well signposted. Round the back of this vast complex, incidentally, you will find the life-support system of the working studios – the casting centre, administration blocks, production and technical services. This is not just a film set: it all happens here, and you may well encounter film and TV crews shooting stars as you wander round the back lots. *Open:* daily from 09.00hrs (closing time varies seasonally).

Visiting Universal Studios
The park is nominally subdivided into six different sections, though these are not very sharply defined, and to see Universal Studios at all efficiently you will need to dodge about quite a bit. You must organise your visit round show schedules and queues, rather than tackle the attractions in straightforward geographical sequence.

When you first enter the park, have a good look at the free guide and map they give you with your ticket, and at the **Production Schedule** posted by the turnstiles. Do not get bogged down by the entrance. Proceed rapidly to the most popular rides, where queues build fast after opening time. Do these first, then organise visits to the various shows that mostly start at around 10.00hrs (**Alfred Hitchcock: The Art of Making Movies** showings begin earlier, from 09.10hrs). Rides which suffer badly from long, slow-moving queues include **The Funtastic World of Hanna–Barbera**, **Kongfrontation**, **Back to the Future**, and **ET**. Make the most of any early energy you have. The main attractions are described in the order in which they are arranged on the ground, not necessarily as numbered (alpabetically) on the plan (page 55) and not the order in which you see them.

The Front Lot

Mostly taken up with practical stuff like lost children and guest relations, though you will find a tempting fudge shop guaranteed to waylay any sweet-toothed child before you have made it to the end of the block. If you did not get a chance for breakfast and are starving, grab a sandwich or pastry at the **Beverly Hills Boulangerie**, but do not hang about. From the main entrance, walk straight ahead up the **Plaza of the Stars**.

Production Central

◆◆◆
THE FUNTASTIC WORLD OF HANNA–BARBERA

Take this in right away if queues do not seem too long. Hanna–Barbera is not some American sit-com heroine you have not caught up with yet, but a composite of the two successful animation cartoonists Bill Hanna and Joe Barbera, creators of such folk heroes as Yogi Bear, the Flintstones, Scooby Doo and, most recently, the Jetsons. It is a flight-simulated ride involving a high-speed chase with Yogi Bear (a poor driver) to rescue a kidnapped child. The visual effects of colour, speed and depth are astonishing and colossally expensive (film technology buffs may drool) and can be slightly sick-making. This attraction is not as cuddly and innocuous as it looks on the video screens as you wait in line. Take the unmoving seats at the front if you get queasy.

◆◆◆
ALFRED HITCHCOCK: THE ART OF MAKING MOVIES

The presentation is a little confusing in parts, but it is a great show if you know and love those old thrillers. The Master of Suspense himself presides in his inimitably ponderous style. First there is a 3-D version of *The Birds* (and you thought the original film was scary enough – wait till those gulls are whirling round the auditorium, pecking your eyes out!). The next part of the show is based on the making of *Psycho*, 'the movie that drove thousands to sponge-baths!' It is introduced on film by a charming and reassuringly normal Anthony Perkins, somewhat older than we remember him at Bates Motel. (Incidentally, he tells us, he didn't do it. The menacingly shrouded figure with the knife was a stand-in while he was rehearsing in New York. A likely tale!)
The audience learns how Hitchcock used 78 separate camera angles to create those

few terrifying seconds in the shower scene, still a classic piece of film-making endlessly dissected by movie hounds. After the tension of the pizzicato violins, it is a relief to learn that the nasty dark stuff washing down the plug-hole is – chocolate syrup! Ketchup just would not come out dark enough in black and white. Audience volunteers and professional actors lightheartedly recreate the famous stabbing scene, and further film-set and suspense techniques are revealed in the third staging area. Afterwards, you can wander out to the shop and buy some Bates Motel soap or hand-towels for your favourite house-guests.

◆
PRODUCTION TOUR AND NICKELODEON STUDIOS
Heading left down Nickelodeon Way you reach a large complex of back-lot sets and studios which can be visited, partly on a guided tram tour. It is mildly interesting if you can hear the bewildering quick-fire commentary, but a lot of it relates to popular US television (especially children's) shows with which foreign visitors may be unfamiliar, and it goes on far too long. However, it gives some behind-the-scenes insights into the complexity and variety of location filming. Learn how carefully those seagull droppings were painted on the (similarly painted) cobblestones, and see the specially created 'swamp' for adventure movies.

◆◆◆
MURDER SHE WROTE MYSTERY THEATER
This zappy multi-stage presentation involving frenzied interaction with the audience is lively and great fun. Angela Lansbury (on film) shows how editors, sound recordists, and camera crews can make or break a show (in this case an episode from the Emmy Award-winning TV whodunnit). Become a temperamental producer, and feel the pressure – time and money are running out. Can you yell 'No, absolutely not!' loud enough to fit the part?

The studio's San Francisco set

UNIVERSAL STUDIOS

New York

You will know you have reached the next set by the architecture, a faithful mock-up of those Manhattan skyscrapers. Within a few hundred square yards you will find Broadway and Greenwich Village, Little Italy and Upper East Side. Here the more egotistical visitor can have a screen test and take home the resulting charismatic video, or be photographed for a magazine cover shot. You can play arcade games, buy 'paranormal' souvenirs, or sling down some protein at **Louie's Italian Restaurant** or **Finnegan's**, a New York Irish bar. There are two main crowd-pullers in this area.

◆◆

GHOSTBUSTERS

This curious show will appeal to Green Slime fans. The 'spooktacular' special effects are certainly remarkable; it is a very costly production. The story line is utter garbage, but the ghosts and the scale of the set are wondrous, involving 2,300 computer cues, 11 tons of liquid nitrogen, and a unique 'now you see it, now you don't' laser system.

◆◆◆

KONGFRONTATION

Everyone has to do this ride. King Kong stalks New York, creating predictable mayhem. You, of course, are helplessly caught in his grip; trapped in an aerial tramway car, your life hangs by a thread as you swing over the East River. The great ape weighs six tons and stands four storeys tall, the largest computer-animated model ever constructed. The sound stage for Kongfrontation is one of the most elaborate in the world, with full-scale helicopter models. At the end of the journey, passengers relive their 'terror' on video, filmed while they were in transit (most of them are laughing!).

Punch-up at the Wild West Show

Hollywood Boulevard

The Beverly Hills and Sunset Boulevard sets house cafés and shops selling Hollywood headgear, sunglasses and movie posters. The main attraction is a gorily impressive foray into the world of special horror effects (the **Gory, Gruesome and Grotesque Horror Make-Up Show**). Not recommended for sensitive plants.

San Francisco/Amity

The large artificial lagoon and its surrounding streets encompass sets of cheerful seasidey architecture, attractive shops and eating places. Just when you thought it was safe to leave the sidewalk, there is that old White Shark , 'Jaws', dangling by the quayside. Other main attractions are two thrill rides and two stunt shows.

EARTHQUAKE – THE BIG ONE

A compelling simulated subway ride through San Francisco when all hell breaks loose, accompanied by an interesting film and demonstration of how these incredibly realistic special effects are achieved.

JAWS

More high-tech special effects as the big fish takes a snap at your excursion boat.

WILD, WILD, WILD WEST STUNT SHOW

Popular show held several times daily in a stadium at the far side of the complex. Lots of hammy stuff with trick sharpshooting, brawling, explosives, jumping off buildings, abseiling down wires, and so on. The audience is warned not to try these things at home, as they may be quite dangerous!

DYNAMITE NIGHTS STUNT SPECTACULAR

This is Universal's big end-of-day bang, an explosive action-packed boat-chase round the lagoon, based on a *Miami Vice* drug-raid scene. It is full of sound and fury, but the action is intermittent, and the main problem is to get a good enough vantage point to see the whole of the show. Unless you are wild about motor-boats, do not bother too much if you miss this. You may be better off commandeering a table at the **Hard Rock Café** before the crowds pour in.

World Expo Center

Several slick eating places, and some very popular rides, including Universal's *pièce de résistance*:

BACK TO THE FUTURE

This suffers somewhat from promotional overkill. By the time you get on this ride (after queueing long and hard), you are so determined it is the biggest thing since Ben Hur that the reality is almost bound to disappoint. Yes, it is exciting, thrilling, technically wizard, using multi-channel surround sound and seven-storey hemispherical screens. But it is only a simulation, and if you have been on a few of these rides you will have an idea what to expect. Nevertheless, theme-parkers, you have to do this one.

ET ADVENTURE
Join Steven Spielberg's lovable alien in a new adventure on a star-bound bicycle traversing redwood forests and cities to the Green Planet and its extraordinary magic flowers. Wonderful special effects. It is a nice ride for children of all ages.

ANIMAL ACTORS STAGE
Remember that advice about never appearing on screen with children and animals? Here the animals have it all their own way. Find out how these furred and feathered stars are trained, and see them strut their stuff. A good show.

Restaurants
There are lots of places to satisfy your appetite quickly during the day. As there is such a lot to see at Universal Studios, it is best not to waste time on a sit-down meal at lunch-time. Graze during the day, then

Meticulous detail on a film set

make sure you have an enjoyable dinner when the park closes. You will need a rest. Interesting light bites among the shakes and burgers include **Café La Bamba**'s Mexican snacks (Hollywood); the **San Francisco Pastry Co**'s luscious cakes and speciality coffees (San Francisco/Amity); and Irish fare and ales at **Finnegan's** (New York). In the evenings, by far the most popular venue is the celebrated **Hard Rock Café**, the largest of its name in the world, shaped like a guitar, cluttered with pop memorabilia (open until 02.00hrs) It is cool, chic, and very crowded. Prices are not cheap, but the food is good with many alternatives to hamburgers. Incidentally, you can dine at the Hard Rock Café without paying theme-park admissions (there is a separate entrance and free car park). If you really cannot stand the look of the queues here, head for the quieter atmosphere of **Lombard's Landing** on the waterfront, where steaks, pasta and seafood are agreeably served in an 1800s San Francisco warehouse setting (reservations advisable, but not always necessary).

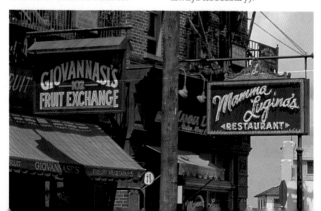

CHURCH STREET STATION

Back in the 1970s this old railroad depot was badly run-down and dilapidated, but a visionary proposal to create a glittery entertainment complex has given Orlando's myriad tourists a valid reason to venture downtown. The core of this mini-theme park is its oldest attraction, the turn-of-the-century-style saloon known as **Rosie O'Grady's Good-Time Emporium**. After the success of this, many other night-spots and restaurants were gradually invented in neighbouring buildings, most recently its ambitious three-storey Victorian shopping centre, known as the **Church Street Exchange** (see **Shopping**, page 91). The enclosed street set, perhaps a hundred yards (90m) long, now houses about a dozen separate attractions. One entrance fee (charge after 17.00hrs only) covers admission to the whole street and all the shows, but you do not have to pay to visit the Exchange shops. The Church Street complex is open from 11.00hrs each day, but the shows happen only during the evenings, so most people arrive towards the end of the day. Especially wild nights at Church Street include Halloween and New Year, when the intended street party atmosphere really takes off. One reason for the success of Church Street Station is the care and quality with which the settings of these wacky dancehalls and eating places have been created. Items have been scavenged from all over the world to decorate and furnish the elaborate fun-palaces: a confessional from a French monastery converted into a phone booth, *fin de siècle* brass chandeliers from a Boston bank, etched mirrors from a Glasgow pub. And yes, it is a real steam train out there. The results are certainly eclectic (indiscriminate, even) but they work. The impression as you walk into any of the attractions is of great richness and glitter; everywhere you look there is something to arouse curiosity. It is fun, imaginative, and pretty!

The stylish Cheyenne Saloon

CHURCH STREET STATION

The entertainments at Church Street are ebullient affairs, and generally the complex appeals to young adults, but there is hardly anything you could not take a child to (minimum age in Phineas Phogg's is 21). The shows start at around 19.00hrs, and are timed so you can catch several in an evening. Most of the restaurants stay open till midnight, a couple of nightspots till 02.00hrs. Any eating or shopping you do in Church Street will be fairly pricey.

To get there, take the Anderson Street Exit 38 from Highway I-4 and follow the signs. There are several places to park.

Open: daily 11.00–02.00hrs. Admission charged after 17.00hrs; reduced for under 13s, free for under 3s.

◆◆◆
ROSIE O'GRADY'S GOOD-TIME EMPORIUM
Dixieland jazz, showboat banjos, and girls with good legs clattering Charlestons or can-cans on the bar-tops recreate an ambience somewhere between the Gay 90s and the Roaring 20s in this brassily ornate saloon, reborn from the shabby old Orlando Hotel. 'Rosie', a Red Hot Momma mistress of ceremonies, makes sure everyone's havin' a real good time. Refreshments include deli-style sandwiches and bizarre cocktails. Show-times start at 19.30hrs.

◆◆
CHEYENNE SALOON AND OPERA HOUSE
The Wild West lives on here in a set lovingly created from gold oak lumber (an old Ohio barn), brilliant stained glass, antique guns and the pews from a Catholic church. Heel-kickin', feet-stompin' shows of Country and Western music, and traditional barbecue fare.

◆
LILI MARLENE'S AVIATOR'S PUB AND RESTAURANT
Aviation memorabilia dangles amid a warm glow of pegged timbers and bevelled glass. Food is hearty ribs, steaks and seafood.

◆
APPLE ANNIE'S COURTYARD
Featuring live music (bluegrass and folk) in a quieter mode, where you may have time to look around at some fine antiques. Natural fruit juices and cocktails.

◆
ORCHID GARDEN BALLROOM
A Victorian fantasy of glass, marble and wrought iron, accompanied by popular hits from the 50s onwards.

◆◆
PHINEAS PHOGG'S BALLOON WORKS
Ballooning memorabilia and high-energy music, popular with a youngish in-crowd. **Nickel Beer** nights on Wednesdays involve 'Happy Hour' prices from 17.30–19.00hrs (5¢ for a beer). Minimum age 21.

◆
CRACKERS OYSTER BAR
A good place to try a bowl of seafood chowder or gumbo with a generously sized glass of Californian white. Downstairs is a well-stocked wine cellar.

Newborn crocodiles, Busch Gardens

BUSCH GARDENS ✓

This massive 300-acre (120-ha) theme park of rides and roller coasters also has over 3,000 real animals of 350 different species, and counts as one of the USA's most important zoos. It plays a significant role in breeding and conserving endangered species. If you can take any more 'family entertainment' after Disney, or indeed if you want an antidote to Disney, you might well make the journey over to Tampa. Busch Gardens is a giant 'Out of Africa' safari park. It first opened in 1959, so is an older attraction than anything at Walt Disney World. That soon becomes apparent: things are just not quite as neat and tidy here – the ponds may be a little clogged with weed, the monorail slightly dilapidated. Its rumbustiously authentic fauna are also distinctly more pungent than the antiseptic animations that inhabit the Disney theme parks.

Practical Details

It is about an hour and a quarter's drive from Walt Disney World to Busch Gardens. From Orlando head west on I-4 towards Tampa, then take I-75. From here take Exit 54 (Fowler Ave) and follow the signs. Busch Gardens is at the intersection of Busch Boulevard and 40th Street, eight miles (13km) north-east of downtown Tampa.

There is a lot to see at Busch Gardens. You need at least a day to see everything, more if you want to allow time for the adjacent water park called **Adventure Island** (separate admission fee and opening times). Plan to arrive as close to opening time as you can. There is a modest parking fee. Take your hat and sun-cream if it is hot: there is a lot of outdoors at Busch Gardens. When you enter the park, check the show times and decide which ones you want to head for. The usual panoply of strollers, wheelchairs, cameras, lost and found offices, and first aid posts are available. The 'house rules' are similar to those in WDW, though here alcohol is more widely available - after all, Anheuser-Busch (the owners) make the stuff! Transport includes a monorail (somewhat less high-tech than Disney's), a quaint steam locomotive, and a cable-car.

Open: daily 09.30–18.00hrs (longer in summer and at holiday times). Not all the shows take place every day. Children under 2 get in free. If you have already visited Sea World or Cypress Gardens you may be able to get a discount – ask at **Guest Relations**.

Visiting Busch Gardens

The park is divided into eight differently themed 'lands', a rather similar structure to the large Disney theme parks.

♦♦♦
MOROCCO

Evident from the Moorish architecture of fancy tiles and castellated walls, this is the first 'land' as you enter from the parking lot. Moroccan crafts and souvenirs are on display, along with dark-eyed snake charmers, a theatre (regular shows of 60s and country music), and the rather unexpected Mystic Sheiks eight-piece brass marching band. The main attraction here, though, is the **Moroccan Palace**, where a spectacular ice-skating show, *Around the World on Ice*, is held four times daily. The acts are excellent and very well rehearsed. Sets flit from Paris to Egypt to South America to Russia, with some lovely costumes. The juggler is particularly watchable, although the contents of his act have no discernible connection with Morocco.

For a quick snack here, try the **Boujad Bakery** (North African pastries). The **Zagora Café** does burgers, deli sandwiches and breakfasts. There is an ice cream parlour too.

♦♦
NAIROBI

There are lots of animals here, including crocodiles and alligators (in separate pens – they don't like each other much), reptiles and fish. Special attractions include elephants having baths, nocturnal animals enjoying their lifestyle in simulated night-time conditions, a petting zoo and an animal nursery, where baby creatures tug at the heartstrings. Nairobi is also a place to pick up the jolly little colonial-looking **Trans-Veldt Railroad** train that chugs round the northern outskirts of the park.

♦
CROWN COLONY

Here you can find the rather un-African Budweiser Clydesdale horses who pull ceremonial drays, and **Crown Colony House**, a full-service restaurant with elaborate colonial Victorian decor. It is one of the most comfortable places for a meal in Busch Gardens, with views over the Serengeti Plain.

♦
SERENGETI PLAIN

This 80-acre (32-ha) expanse of flat Florida countryside does not really look too much like African savannah, but the animals help. Giraffes, antelope, gazelles, ostriches and camels lope about on the plains. Rare species like black rhino are being successfully bred here. To see the animals, take the skyride cable car, monorail, or steam locomotive.

◆◆
TIMBUKTU

A fairground in a desert trading post atmosphere. Thrill rides include the sickening **Phoenix** boat swing, the alarming loop-the-loop **Scorpion** roller coaster, and the whirling **Sandstorm**. The **Dolphin Theater** is here (regular dolphin shows), plus **Das Festhaus** where food and entertainment is of the Germanic variety. Games, shops and a juice-bar are additional diversions.

◆
CONGO

At the northwest corner of the park a few more animals are in evidence among the rides. On **Claw Island** several beautiful Bengal tigers disdainfully regard their audience from a setting of rocks and waterfalls, occasionally giving them an elegant aquatic show as they plunge into their moat. Best things to do here are the **Congo River Rapids** (white-water raft ride) and the **Python** roller-coaster, a yellow serpent that convolutes its passengers through two complete 360-degree spirals. It is fairly alarming, but does not last long.

◆
STANLEYVILLE

This continues the African theme with the **Stanley Falls** (log flume ride) and the **Tanganyika Tidal Wave**, where screaming passengers plummet down a slide into water and completely drench themselves and any bystanders. There is a shopping bazaar and a variety show in the **Stanleyville Theater**.

◆
BIRD GARDENS

One of the older sections of the park, some parts of it are looking almost nostalgically dated now. **Eagle Canyon** ('natural' habitat for golden and bald eagles) and a free-flight walk-through aviary. There is also a koala exhibit and the **World of Birds** show in the **Bird Theater** (theatrical parrots and obedient birds of prey). Commentary is a bit saccharine, but it is friendly and reasonably educational.

◆
ANHEUSER–BUSCH BREWERY

This is the tall blocky concrete and metallic structure you may have been wondering about at intervals round the park. You can tour it, at your own pace, and learn lots of worthy things about the company, including their commitment to recyling and the fight against alcoholism. Then you can try some of the stuff free at Hospitality House. Close by, for the predilection of children, is Dwarf Village.

Bar-top entertainment

KENNEDY SPACE ✓ CENTER

What's in a name?

John F Kennedy will be for ever linked with the US space programme. It was his determination to set a man on the moon by the end of the 1960s that provided the initial momentum for those many space missions which culminated in the triumphant Apollo moon landing in 1969. When Kennedy was assassinated in 1963, the whole of the Cape Canaveral peninsula was renamed Cape Kennedy in his memory. Ten years later this decision was confusingly rescinded, and the old name was restored. Cape Kennedy no longer exists. Cape Canaveral, an Air Force station where long-range military rockets were tested after World War II, is the historical site of the early NASA (National Aeronautics and Space Administration) space launches. It is a jutting peninsula of low-lying coastal marshlands, separated from the Florida mainland by two meandering rivers enclosing Merritt Island. The Kennedy Space Center, the modern launch-site for the US space programme, is based on the northern part of this island, and is now Florida's third most popular visitor attraction.

Getting There

It is about an hour's drive from Orlando to the east coast, most

A bus demonstrates the rockets' size

painlessly achieved on the Beeline Expressway which leads past the International Airport. Have some loose change handy for several toll gates. Follow signs for Kennedy Space Center (State Roads 407/405), not Cape Canaveral.

Practical Details

To see everything at the Kennedy Space Center, allow the best part of a day. It is best to arrive early.

Open: 09.00hrs until dusk. There is a lot of hard information (eye-popping statistics, measurements, space facts and figures) to grasp if you are interested, but even if you have only a mild curiosity about the US space programme, the chances are that a visit to the Kennedy Space Center and the military airforce base of Cape Canaveral will enthuse you. Somehow, actually seeing the launch-pad, standing cheek to fuselage with a real Saturn V rocket, makes the great space adventure vivid in a way satellite television never can. Both parking, and admission to **Spaceport USA** (the visitor information centre), are completely free, which must make it one of the best sightseeing bargains in the whole of Florida.

The Spaceport is merely an appetite-whetter for the real stuff of the Kennedy Space Center. To see that, you have to join one of the comfortable, air-conditioned bus tours that leave at frequent intervals to tour the site. There are two bus tours: Red and Blue. Both cost the same; both are worth doing,

with excellent commentaries, boggling statistics and frequent camera stops. As well as the bus tours, there is also a charge for entry to a couple of excellent films (and of course for any food or souvenirs you buy). None of these attractions is at all overpriced, and there are reductions for children aged 3–11.

Despite the futuristic subject matter, however, facilities at the Space Center are not as streamlined or high-tech as at Walt Disney World, nor are there as many staff in attendance to handle crowds. On busy days film shows or tours may get booked up quickly, so as soon as you arrive it is a good idea to reserve a place on whichever bus tours you want, and buy tickets for the IMAX films, *The Dream is Alive*, and *Blue Planet*. Decide whether you are going to eat before or after the tours: they last around two hours, and you will not have a chance to stop for food on the way.

◆◆
MERRITT ISLAND NATIONAL WILDLIFE REFUGE

The road to the Space Center leads over a causeway across the Indian River to Merritt Island, an important nature reserve extraordinarily rich in wildlife (see also page 86). Although it is hard to believe in this high-tech, top-security area, there are more rare and endangered species here than anywhere else on the US mainland. Herons, egrets, ospreys and eagles could well be whirling about with Cape

Canaveral's military jets within easy distance of your car. When rockets periodically roar into orbit with such awe-inspiring force, these blasé creatures scarcely bat an eye. The 7-mile (11km) **Blackpoint Wildlife Drive** through the Merritt Island Refuge enables you to see many different species, and there is a visitor centre. Look out for slow-moving, slow-thinking armadillos on the road. They are often squashed by vehicles.

SPACEPORT USA

By a lagoon near the entrance you will notice the Astronaut's Memorial, a vast 'Space Mirror' honouring the 15 US astronauts who have died in space accidents – a rotating mirror projects their names up to the sky, so that they appear to float among the clouds. Entering the Spaceport is like stumbling into a lunar parking lot. Life-size replicas of modules and skylabs, and some actual space hardware, stand to attention in the open-air **Rocket Garden**, each neatly labelled with a fact-filled information plaque: how big, how fast, how long, how often, and the like. You can clamber aboard the monstrous Ambassador orbiter and see how little elbow-room NASA astronauts have on board a shuttle flight.

Inside the various buildings on the Spaceport you will find cinemas showing space films (including the film, *The Boy from Mars*, a view of life in the 21st century) and many displays and information boards of space

equipment, models, video screens, and so on. A bit of moon rock is proudly displayed.

You could spend any amount of time in here sorting out all those Mercury, Gemini, and Apollo missions. There is some interesting stuff on the Russian Soyuz programme too.

A fairly recent addition, **Satellites and You**, is a 55-minute walk through a simulated space station, with audiovisuals demonstrating how satellites affect life on Earth.

One thing definitely not to miss, however, is the IMAX film *The Dream is Alive*, filmed by astronauts circling the Earth, skilfully narrated by Walter Cronkite, and shown on a screen the size of a five-storey building. The visual effects are absolutely stunning. To recover from this experience, you could head for the **Orbit Cafeteria** and retrieve your hot dog from a revolving carousel.

BLUE BUS TOUR

This takes a more historic perspective, showing visitors the Cape Canaveral base where the earliest space flights were launched.

RED BUS TOUR

This is far more popular, covering the modern launch-site and the administrative and operations buildings. You will learn a bit about the astronauts' training programme, experience an exciting simulated launch (Propellants Pressurised, Forward Arm

The giant IMAX screen at the Galaxy Center is compelling

Retracted, Commit, LIFT OFF), and see a real lunar module – a curious contraption sporting metal instruments at all angles and spider legs draped in yellow tinfoil. On film, watch Neil Armstrong bouncing happily over the moon's surface.

Outside again, you head for the massive **Vehicle Assembly Building** (largest roofed structure in the world, capable of holding three and a half dismantled Empire State Buildings). Then gawp at the mammoth **Crawler Transporter**, the largest vehicle in the world, which at its maximum stately pace of 1mph (1.6kph) takes about seven hours to carry rockets the short distance to the launch site. Amazingly, a couple of rare bald eagles nest along this

route, presumably regarding the space-craft as some sort of kindred aerial species.

You get a close-up of a vast Saturn V rocket, like the one that carried *Apollo* to the Moon, and finally a glimpse of the launch platform itself, where there just might be a shuttle spacecraft being readied for action. You would have to be very, very cool not to be impressed.

◆◆
SEEING A LAUNCH

If you are seriously interested in the space programme, you might try timing your visit to coincide with an actual launch. Obviously schedules may easily be affected by weather or technical hitches, so it is not worth rearranging your plans too drastically. But if there is a chance, the drill is to head out the night before (stay somewhere in Titusville or

Cocoa Beach), get up hideously early, and prepare for a long wait with countless other space techno-freaks. Ask the information centre at the Spaceport for a handout on where to find the best viewpoints, and so on. (You could, of course, watch a launch more conveniently on TV from any motel room, but that would lack mettle!)

◆

UNITED STATES ASTRONAUT HALL OF FAME

This new attraction is under separate management from the Space Center and charges its own admission fees (almost half-price for 3–12-year-olds). You will spot it before you reach the Space Center, on NASA Parkway (State Road 405) at Titusville.

Inside the Hall of Fame, multimedia presentations (video footage and recorded interviews, personal memorabilia, films, models and diagrams) portray the lives and achievements of the first American astronauts, including John Glenn, Alan Shepard, and the ill-fated *Challenger* crew. Lots of hero-worship, but after all, these were heroes.
Open: daily 08.00–dusk. Closed: Christmas Day, and certain launch dates.
In the same building is the **US Space Camp**, where visitors can experience hands-on astronaut training. Children bunk out of school for five-day courses to become fully fledged spacepersons with the one-sixteenth Gravity Chair, the Multi-Axis Simulator and the Space Shuttle Orbiter Simulator. On top of the building is an **Observation Deck**, from where you can see the Spaceport area – and perhaps even see a live space shuttle launch if you are very lucky.

WHAT ELSE TO SEE IN ORLANDO

Some (but not all) of these sights are pretty small beer, a fact not always evident from their admission charges. It is worth planning ahead and being selective about what really interests you, or you could end up frustrated, wasting a lot of time and money.

INTERNATIONAL DRIVE AREA

◆◆

MEL FISHER'S WORLD OF TREASURE

8586 Palm Parkway (Exit 27 off I-4, right two blocks)
An attractively laid out exhibition of artefacts recovered by Mel Fisher's salvage team from a fleet of Spanish galleons wrecked in a storm off the Florida Keys in 1622. Gold ingots, emeralds, swords and various bits of ship's tackle are on display, much encrusted from their centuries of submersion in salt water.
There is a short film, which describes in fascinating detail the discovery – and recovery – of the treasure hoard, which took many years to trace, identify and document.
Open: daily 10.00–23.00hrs.

◆
MYSTERY FUN HOUSE
5767 Major Boulevard
Mild frissons of terror with the
Egyptian Tomb, the Wizard's 15
Chambers of Surprise, the
mirror maze, and the Starbase
Omega laser game (additional
charge). After that, play with the
pinball machines and video
games by the exit. Mini-golf is
also available.
Open: daily 10.00–22.00hrs.

Restaurants
Among the tacky fast-food
chains and diners is a good
selection of really superior
eating places. **The Peabody
Hotel**, 9801 International Drive
(tel: 352 4000) has three good
restaurants, all very different,
but all pricey: **Dux** is smart,
formal and intimate, with one of
the highest Triple A accolades
in Orlando (cooking a marriage
of American and oriental

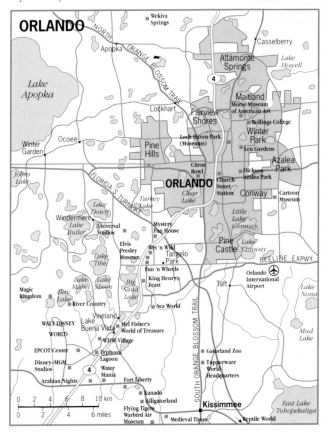

WHAT ELSE TO SEE

styles); **Capriccio** is in North Italian trattoria style; the **B-Line Diner** is a popular 50s-style café/bar open all day. **Ming Court**, 9188 International Drive (tel: 351 9988) is the classiest Chinese around this area, with dishes of all the great styles: Mandarin, Szechuan, Hunan and Cantonese. **Ming Gardens**, under the same management at No 6432, is more moderately priced (tel: 352 8044). Another interesting ethnic experience is **Phoenician** (Middle Eastern specialities: *meze* lets you try lots) at The Marketplace, 7600 Dr Phillips Boulevard (tel: 345 1001). In the same street is one of Orlando's best Italian restaurants, **Christini's**, 7600 Dr Phillips Boulevard (tel: 345 8770). **Siam Orchid** is a well-regarded Thai restaurant, 7575 Republic Drive (tel: 351 3935). **Royal Orleans** does a splendid range of Louisiana Cajun-style dishes like shrimp and crawfish Mercado Mediterranean Village, 8445 International Drive (tel: 352 8200).

LAKE WALES

About an hour's drive south-west of Orlando is a peaceful wooded area of lakes and citrus groves, popular for fishing, camping and boating. Head west on I-4 in the Tampa direction, then take US27 South.

BOK TOWER GARDENS

Three miles (5km) north of Lake Wales. Follow signs along Alt 27 from US27. (Map, pages 16–17.)
The 255-foot (78m) **Singing Tower** of pink and grey marble makes a landmark for miles

around. Crowning Florida's highest point (at about 300 feet (91m) above sea level that is not saying much!), it forms the centrepiece of a splendid 128-acre (52-ha) garden of azaleas and other flowering shrubs, which was donated to the American people in 1929 by the Dutch immigrant writer, Edward W. Bok. The tower contains an elaborate carillon of 57 bronze bells which serenade visitors with a great mix of melodies every half-hour (special 45-minute recital at 15.00hrs).
There are no rides or shows or blaring microphones in this garden: just birdsong and the sound of bells. It is a marvellous antidote to the fevered artificiality of the theme parks, and entrance is very cheap by Orlando standards (under-12s free).
Open: daily 08.00–17.00hrs.

CYPRESS GARDENS

Off US27 near Winter Haven – follow signs.
(Map, pages 16–17.)
A much larger and more commercialised attraction than Bok Tower Gardens, owned by Disney's great rivals Anheuser–Busch (who also-run Sea World and Busch Gardens). It has the distinction of being Orlando's oldest theme park, predating Disney by over 30 years. Created from swampland in 1936, it consists of 223 acres (90 ha) of carefully manicured gardens, shows, restaurants, shops and rides. The **'Mum'** (chrysanthemum) **Festival** every November is as showily

spectacular as the gorgeous southern belles who embellish the gardens in their hooped petticoats. Ancillary diversions include performing birds, an eye-catching waterski and microlight show, boat rides through the gardens, a model railroad, antique carousel, Kodak's Island in the Sky (a circular viewing platform raised and lowered periodically by a hydraulic lift), and 8,000 species of plants from 75 countries. Though gaudy in parts, the gardens are undoubtedly well kept, with lots of botanical interest. Less plant-minded folk will also have plenty to see and do. Admission charges are quite expensive, so allow time to make the most of everything the attraction offers. (If you visit other Busch attractions, such as Sea World, you can get a discount.) During the shows the atmosphere can be distractingly noisy.
Open: daily 09.00–18.00hrs (extended in holiday period).

Restaurants
Chalet Suzanne Restaurant and Country Inn (see also **Accommodation**, page 101), between Bok Tower and the Cypress Gardens just off US27 (exit 17A), has an unusual and excellent restaurant. It is well worth booking ahead for lunch or dinner if you are planning a trip out to the Lake Wales area, though the restaurant alone merits the journey. Specialities include Chicken Suzanne, Rum Cream Pie, and the legendary Soup Romaine, which the Apollo astronauts sampled on their moon-landing flight (tel: 813 676 6011, toll-free 800 288 6011)).

The Cypress Gardens are Orlando's oldest theme park

WHAT ELSE TO SEE

LAKE COUNTY

FLORIDA CITRUS TOWER
On US27 in Clermont, 45 minutes west of Orlando.
(Map, pages 16-17.)
This is about as high as you can get in Florida without a hot-air balloon. The observation tower surveys the citrus groves, which you can also tour on foot or by tram, and you may sample the produce in candied or marmalade form. The surrounding complex includes many other attractions. Under-9s go free. *Open:* daily 08.00–18.00hrs (restaurant 07.00–21.00hrs). Nearby on US27 North is the **Lakeridge Winery** – free daily tours, plus the chance to taste some of Florida's local offerings.

NORTHERN ORLANDO

As you leave Orlando city on I-4 heading north-east towards Daytona, you pass the museum park of **Loch Haven**, a smart residential suburb called **Winter Park**, and the historic riverside community of **Sanford**. Further out are the rural resorts of **Wekiva Springs** and old Floridian villages like **Mount Dora** and **Apopka**, popular with campers, walkers and lovers of the Great Outdoors. Also in this direction is the spiritualist camp of **Cassadaga**.

LOCH HAVEN PARK
Take Exit 43 off I-4 (Princeton Street), then head a mile east
A lakeview landscaped park (picnics, kite-flyers, and so on). Three small museums and some pleasant gardens are worth a glance if you're passing, though not a special detour.

Orange County Historical Museum
Somewhat jumbled exhibits on Orange County's early development, at 812 East Rollins Street.
Open: Tuesday to Friday 09.00–17.00hrs; Saturday and Sunday 12.00–17.00hrs.
At the rear is Orlando's oldest standing fire station, dating from 1926. Early fire-fighting vehicles and equipment, photographs and murals.
Open: Tuesday to Friday 10.00–16.00hrs; Saturday and Sunday 13.00–17.00hrs. *Closed:* Monday.

Orlando Museum of Art
Undergoing renovation, this museum on 2416 North Mills Avenue contains a fine collection of pre-Columbian art from South America, 19th- and 20th-century American art, African artefacts, and periodically changing exhibitions.
Open: Tuesday to Thursday 09.00–7.00hrs; Friday 09.00–19.30; Saturday 10.00–17.00hrs; Sunday 12.00–17.00hrs. *Closed:* Monday.

Orlando Science Center
810 East Rollins Street
The centre displays educational exhibits for children, including plenty to touch and experiment with. The **John Young Planetarium** hosts daily starshows and cosmic

A Tiffany window, Morse Museum

concerts at weekends
(additional charge).
Open: Monday to Thursday
09.00–17.00hrs;
Friday 09.00– 21.00hrs;
Saturday 12.00– 21.00hrs;
Sunday 12.00–17.00hrs.

Leu Gardens
1730 N. Forest Ave
Fifty seven acres of winding
paths through camellias,
azaleas, rose gardens,
woodland and palms. The floral
clock is one focal point; so too is
Leu House Museum (1730
North Forest Avenue), a turn of
the century Floridian farmhouse.
Museum open: Tuesday to
Saturday 10.00–16.00hrs;
Sunday and Monday
13.00–16.00hrs. *Grounds open*
daily, 09.00–17.00hrs.

Restaurants
If you are downtown, head for
**Townsend's Fish House and
Tavern** (same management as
the **Apopka Townsend's**)
where a yuppy crowd gathers
for snacky things to accompany
a good range of wines by the
glass, 35 West Michigan Street
(tel: 422 5560). A little further

north, **Café on the Park** serves
steak, shellfish and Sunday
brunch overlooking sparkling
Lake Eola, 151 East Washington
Street (tel: 841 3220).

◆◆
WINTER PARK
This posh district, formerly a *fin
de siècle* winter resort for the
wealthy, has a lovely setting on
a string of lakes, now
surrounded by millionaire
mansions. Characterised by
smart 'European-style' shops,
art galleries, up-market
restaurants, chic bars and one
of Orlando's most elegant
hotels, Winter Park is a pleasant
and relaxing place to visit, or
even to base yourself for a few
days. It has a theatre and two
small art museums (the **Morse
Museum** – see below – and the
Cornell Fine Arts Museum, in
Rollins College).

Morse Museum of American Art
133 East Welbourne Avenue
Despite the attempts of the
curator to widen the appeal of

WHAT ELSE TO SEE

this charming little museum, the prize contents are undoubtedly the glorious Tiffany mosaic windows and art nouveau glass. Much of this was rescued from Laurelton Hall, Tiffany's Long Island home, after a disastrous fire. Iridescent blue vases are among the most eye-catching pieces.
Open: Tuesday to Saturday 09.30–16.00hrs; Sunday 13.00–16.00hrs.
Closed: Monday.

Park Avenue
A tempting street for luxury, novelty or book shopping (see page 91), with a peaceful park of fountains and palms. The **Park Plaza Hotel** and its excellent restaurant are here (see below). Most shops open from 10.00hrs.

Scenic Boat Tour
An hour-long cruise through lakes and canals, with wildlife (ospreys and snakebirds), luxury houses and the Mediterranean-style **Rollins College** campus. Daily tours from Osceola lakeshore, every hour from 10.00 to 16.30hrs (tel: 644 4056).

*The elegant **Grand Romance**, on the river at Sanford*

Restaurants
Winter Park has a classier collection of restaurants and bars than just about anywhere else in Orlando, so try to eat here if you visit. One of the best and most famous eating places is the restaurant of the Park Plaza Hotel, the **Park Plaza Gardens**, 319 Park Avenue South (tel: 645 2475). In a conservatory setting of lush vegetation you can enjoy classic continental cooking. They are good on seafood, and Sunday brunch (11.00–15.00hrs) is something of an institution. Vying with it for the top end of the market is the beautifully decorated **La Belle Verrière**, full of gorgeous Tiffany stained glass. Classic French, with local ingredients like catfish; 142 Park Avenue South (tel: 645 3377).
Le Cordon Bleu has a good range of well-prepared meat and seafood, plus a vegetarian option; 537 West Fairbanks (tel: 647 7575). **Park Avenue Grille** serves seafood, prime ribs and

steaks amid tiles, plants and brass fittings; piano trio in the evenings; 358 Park Avenue North (tel: 647 4556).

If you are in an Italian mood, you could try **Baby Nova**, an inexpensive spin-off from the larger restaurant Villa Nova next door – bright lights and granite-look tables at 839 North Orlando Avenue (tel: 644 2060) – or the branch of **Olive Garden** (no pun intended) on Park Avenue South.

For sheer fun, **Bubbalou's Bodacious BBQ** dishes up hot fast food on picnic tables beneath dangling baseball caps, 1471 Lee Road (tel: 628 1212).

♦♦
SANFORD
(Map, pages 16-17.)
This little community played an interesting role in the local citrus industry, and still retains a few buildings that in Florida count as historic. Its river and lakeshore location now make it a tourist centre, particularly for regattas and cruises. If you need a base up here, there is a handily placed **Holiday Inn** right on the waterfront. Take Exit 51 from I-4, then head five lights east into Sanford.

Rivership *Grand Romance*
433 North Palmetto Avenue, by the marina
Leisurely dining cruises down the St John's River on this nostalgic-looking sidewheeler paddle steamer (built in 1989!). Daily and evening sailings with food and music, dancing Friday and Saturday evenings (tel: 321 5091, toll free 800-423 7401). Cruises last three or four hours.

Restaurants
For a lunchtime snack, you could try **Christo's** at 107 West 1st Street (tel: 322 3443), a Greek-deli diner with everything from snacks to full meals: filling soups, spinach in filo pastry, and so on.

♦
CASSADAGA
Take Exit 54 from I-4, then county road 4139. (Map, pages 16-17.)
Definitely different, an excursion to the Spiritualist Camp is popular on Sundays. A community of varied mediums has settled in a wooded clearing. Visitors are welcome to turn up any day for psychic readings of palms, Tarot cards, crystal balls, and spiritual counselling. Rates start from about $20. You can either wander round the houses looking at the signboards and beating on doors, or head for the bookshop for information on who is in session that day.

♦
SILVER SPRINGS
Exit 69 off I-75, one mile (1.6km) east of Ocala on SR40. (Map, pages 16-17.)
Popular with outdoor enthusiasts, the area offers jungle cruises, trips in glass-bottomed boats, Jeep safaris, and crystal-clear springs that discharge around 500 million gallons (2,275 million litres) of water a day. Animals from six continents, petting zoo, animal shows, dinosaur exhibits, water park, picnic sites, camping, etc. *Open:* daily, 09.00–17.00hrs (extended hours in summer and holidays).

Restaurants

If you are heading this far north, catch a meal at one of the local resorts. Several are worth a special excursion. **Jordan's Grove** at 1300 South Orlando Avenue, Maitland (tel: 628 0020, not Mondays) is a fine old house with ambitious game, veal, and lamb dishes as well as many simpler choices, with interesting American wines. Nearby, at 9495 South US Highway 17–92 (tel: 831 0442) the **Chesapeake Crab House** serves, who'd have guessed, crab!

Maison & Jardin, the 'Mason Jar', is another converted mansion with white arches and lovely garden views. International dishes are served with panache; 430 South Wymore Road, Altamonte Springs (tel: 862 4410).

In Apopka village, at 604 East Main Street, **Historic Townsend's Plantation**, a splendid Victorian mansion, has satisfying southern specialities such as coconut-fried shrimp, Cajun alligator tail and, of course, fried chicken (tel: 880 1313). High teas are terrific (15.00–17.00hrs, not Sundays).

SOUTHERN ORLANDO

Heading east from Walt Disney World on Highway 192 takes you through the Kissimmee belt of unlovely commercial development, but there are several minor attractions in this direction, including many shopping malls and dinner-show venues (see **Shopping**, page 90, and **Nightlife**, page 102).

◆

XANADU – HOME OF THE FUTURE

4800 Irlo Bronson Memorial Highway

Tomorrow's domestic world – 15 rooms of sculptured walls and computer-controlled gadgetry.

Open: 10.00–22.00hrs.

◆

OLD TOWN, KISSIMMEE

A bright spot in this otherwise ghastly sprawl: a pleasantly designed complex of speciality shops, restaurants and small museums in an 'Old Florida' architectural pastiche of brick streets and ornate shopfronts. Rock and roll fans should head for the **Elvis Presley Museum**, or the 50s-style nightclub, **Wolfman Jacks**, at 5770 Irlo Bronson Memorial Highway.

Open: daily 10.00–22.00hrs.

GATORLAND

14501 South Orange Blossom Trail (US441)

Probably not for animal lovers, despite the strenuous emphasis on 'conservation, education and research'. Alligators that once plagued the swampy cattle ranches of Florida are now farmed for their mottled skins and, as a by-product, their meat. Here you can see lots of alligators of all sizes: hatchlings to leathery 80-year olds. Even cuddle one if you fancy it (jaws carefully taped!). 'Gator-wrestlin' demonstrations and 'Gator Jumparoo' shows are held several times a day by ex-'crackers' (Floridian cow-hands). This is not particularly cruel, just intensely irritating to the somnolent reptiles who would rather bask unmolested and give their marble-sized brains a rest. A swamp walk gives you a less artificial view of the creatures, and an observation tower over part of the farm gives a good idea of an alligator's natural habitat, in other words, a picture of central Florida before the theme parks arrived. Then you get to eat an alligator (it's better than the other way round), and if your wallet and scruples permit, you can buy alligator products (cowboy boots are very expensive; tins of gator chowder less so). *Open:* daily, spring and summer 08.00–20.00hrs; autumn and winter 08.00– 18.00hrs.

◆
TUPPERWARE WORLD HEADQUARTERS
Next to Gatorland on US441 South
Self-guided tours every half-hour through the plush offices, with a short film on the manufacturing process, and displays of the full range of Tupperware products. You can, of course, order it here, but there is no high-pressure sales talk. There is also a collection of food containers from the Egyptians to the present day. Tours are free.
Open: weekdays 09.00– 16.00hrs.

◆
REPTILE WORLD SERPENTARIUM
Four miles (6.5km) east of St Cloud on US192
Not for snake phobics. Self-guided tours take you past 60

reptilian species from Florida and the rest of the world. Watch the venom being extracted for biomedical research at 11.00, 14.00 and 17.00hrs.
Open: Tuesday to Sunday 09.00–17.30hrs. *Closed:* Monday and September.

Restaurants
Gary's Duck Inn at 3974 South Orange Blossom Trail (tel: 843 0270), goes in for seafood, not poultry, and has been practising longer than most folks in Orlando. **Le Coq au Vin** is, naturally, French, friendly and highly competent (rainbow trout, Long Island duck, frog's legs, goat's cheese), 4800 South Orange Avenue (tel: 851 6980). **Epicurean Restaurant** has gourmet Greek stuff and wicked pastries, 7900 East Colonial Drive (tel: 277 2881).

WATER PARKS
Nicer from the setting and landscaping point of view are unquestionably WDW's Typhoon Lagoon and River Country (see pages 49–50). If adrenalin is what counts, you may prefer those below. Note that although lifeguards are present at all times, back and neck injuries are not unknown. Observe all warning notices and instructions carefully.

◆
WATER MANIA
6073 West Irlo Bronson Memorial Highway (US192)
A 38-acre site of chutes and flumes, surf lagoons, wooded picnic grounds, mini-golf courses, and Anaconda raft rides. There is also an 8,100-sq-foot (752-sq-metre) maze.

WHAT ELSE TO SEE

Splash out at Wet'n Wild

Open: daily June–August 09.30–
20.30hrs; March–May and
September–November
10.00–17.00hrs.

◆◆
WET'N WILD
*6200 International Drive (Exit
30A South off I-4)*
Unmistakably artificial tubes

and slides squirm into huge
pools, at this exciting 25-acre
(10-ha) water park. Look out for
the alarming **Black Hole –** a
headlong Cresta Run through
darkness.
Open: daily but variably
depending on season; 09.00–
23.00hrs max; 10.00–17.00hrs
min. Discount admission
operates late in day; under-3s
go free all day.

Peace and Quiet

Countryside and Wildlife around Orlando by Paul Sterry

Few holiday destinations can rival Orlando for the sheer scale of tourist attractions, and Walt Disney World offers more than enough to satisfy many of those who visit central Florida. However, there is another side to Orlando, and those prepared to step aside from the familiar routes will discover that the surrounding area has superb natural locations which are rich in wildlife.

Wekiva Springs State Park

This wooded park lies 18 miles (29km) northwest of Orlando and is an ideal spot for combining peace and quiet with birdwatching. Take route US441 from Orlando as far as Apopka, and then head west on route 436. The entrance is signposted off to the left. Park in designated areas and walk the trails and paths through the open pine woodland looking for birds such as bobwhite quails, small gamebirds that are usually seen in parties of half a dozen or so. You should also keep a sharp lookout for red-shouldered hawks, woodpeckers and warblers.

Kelly County Park

This park is contiguous with Wekiva Springs State Park. Take US441 as far as Apopka and then head north on route 435 until you see the park entrance on your right. Look for woodland birds and mammals such as squirrels in the pine woodland.

Audubon House

Audubon House, in Maitland, is the headquarters of the Florida Audubon Society, the State's leading bird study and

The green heron is a year-round resident of Florida

PEACE AND QUIET

American alligator

conservation organisation.
Information about birdwatching
in the Orlando district can be
obtained here. There is also a
bird of prey care and
rehabilitation centre. The house
is on Lake Avenue (route 438A).

Moss County Park

An ideal spot for birdwatching,
this park is 20 miles south of
Orlando and can be reached by
turning south off the Beeline
Expressway (route 528) on to
route 15 and driving for about 3
miles (5km). Look for woodland
birds and sandhill cranes in the
grassy wetlands and open pine
forest. There are trails within
the park itself.

Lake Monroe

Lake Monroe lies near Sanford,
to the north of Orlando. To
reach it take I-4 north from the
city and turn off on route 17,
heading south for a couple of
miles. The shores of the lake
can be seen from the road –
look for ducks, egrets and
herons, especially during the
winter months. Adjacent to Lake
Monroe is the **Central Florida
Zoological Park**, on route 17. In
addition to the captive animals
and birds, native wild birds can

be found in abundance in and around the swampy areas.
If you drive north on route 17 from Lake Monroe, crossing I-4, you will see **Blue Springs State Recreation Area** signposted to the right. It is good for woodland and water birds as well as the occasional manatee. Further north still on route 17 is **Lake Woodruff National Wildlife Refuge** (turn off at Deleon Springs). This is a superb area for water birds.

Lake Jessup

Lake Jessup lies north of Orlando, close to Sanford. Head north on route 17 from the city and take route 46 east just before you reach Sanford. The

Vultures

Almost anywhere you drive in central Florida, you are likely to see vultures. They often circle overhead and will even visit roadsides in search of animal road casualties. Two species are found in Florida. The black vulture is, as its name suggests, largely black and in flight has broad wings and a comparatively short tail. The turkey vulture also has black plumage but the head is bald and red in colour. In flight, turkey vultures have long wings with a trailing paler margin and a relatively long tail. Sometimes vultures can be seen circling over towns and cities – even Orlando. Although they are bold when it comes to feeding, they are shy birds when nesting, and the nests themselves are seldom seen.

American Alligators

Once persecuted for their skin and because they are perceived as a threat to man, alligators have staged something of a comeback in recent years. They can now be found in many of Florida's waterways and are an interesting, if somewhat awesome feature of the native wildlife. Alligators lay their eggs in sandy banks but spend much of their time in water. They feed mainly on fish but will also take water birds if the opportunity arises. It is not uncommon to see alligators exceeding 10 feet (3m) in length these days – these are probably more than 20 years old.

road passes close to the northern margin of the lake where the marshy habitat is home to birds such as egrets, herons, rails and ducks – look from the bridge. Nearby **Mullet Lake Park** can be reached if you continue east on route 46 for a short while and turn left into Osceola Road. Woodland birds and insect life abound in this tropical oak 'hammock' and the marshes and fields are also full of birds.

Lake Tohopekaliga

This extensive lake lies to the south of Orlando, not far from Kissimmee. From Kissimmee, head south on route 17 and then turn off on route 531. At Overstreet Road, turn left towards the lake shore. Look for egrets, herons, bald eagles, ducks and pelicans.

PEACE AND QUIET

Merritt Island National Wildlife Refuge

On a trip to the John F Kennedy Space Center and Cape Canaveral, visitors who are interested in wildlife should not miss the Merritt Island National Wildlife Refuge. This vast area of lagoons, freshwater and brackish marshes and mangroves – more than 140,000 acres in all – offers some of the best birdwatching in Florida. The coastal scenery, although flat, provides a pleasant setting for anyone intent on a seaside stroll.

To reach the refuge, take route 402 from Titusville across to Merritt Island. Almost anywhere can be good for wildlife but the following spots may be particularly productive.

Having crossed to Merritt Island, ignore the right fork (Beach Road) and continue to the **Blackpoint Wildlife Drive**, a loop road where you can use

Snowy egret

Snowy Egret

Even the smallest ponds, ditches or marshes in central Florida are likely to host birds such as herons and egrets, which thrive on the abundant frogs and fishes. Among the most attractive and distinctive of these is the snowy egret, an aptly named bird with pure white plumage. In the breeding season it develops long plumes on its head, and at all times it has black legs with contrasting yellow toes and shins. Snowy egrets are patient fishers, wading slowly through the shallows until their prey comes within reach. In common with many of Florida's other birds, they are curiously indifferent to people, and can often be watched at extremely close range without being disturbed.

your car as a hide. Then retrace your tracks and follow Beach Road to the **Canaveral National Seashore** where you can look for waders, gulls and terns. Retrace your route again along Beach Road and follow signs to the Visitor Center for information about the refuge. As an alternative, you may wish to visit the nearby **Ulumay Wildlife Refuge**. From Cocoa take route 520 off US route 1 and cross the bridge on to Merritt Island. Turn north towards Sykes Creek Park and stop at the refuge. This is a superb area for herons, egrets, ibises, waders, terns and warblers, and a nature trail affords superb views of the area.

Practical

This section (with the yellow band) includes food, drink, shopping, accommodation, nightlife, tight budget, special events etc.

FOOD AND DRINK

Say 'Florida' to most people and the first thing that springs to mind is – oranges. About 25 per cent of the world's crop is produced here, and about 95 per cent of the total production of concentrated orange juice. Citrus fruits are stacked up in huge outlets by the roadside for passers-by. Try tangelos (a juicy hybrid), pineapple oranges, pink grapefruit, and Persian limes. Citrus juice is always available at breakfast (though little seems freshly squeezed), and you can also buy citrus jams, marmalades, candy, even citrus wine at roadside factory outlets. Florida also grows other types of fruit and vegetables, notably kumquats, strawberries and sweet corn. Once a great cattle-rearing state, cattle are still important and prime rib steak still features on many a Floridian menu.
Seafood, though, is its main gastronomic staple. Even in central Florida you can find excellent fish restaurants. Clams, rock shrimp (langostino), lobster, crawfish,

pompano and scamp (flaky white fish), mullet, oysters, scallops and stone crabs are common specialities. Fresh palm hearts are a local delicacy.
The range of food available in Orlando is less interesting than the ethnic variety and number of establishments suggests. Much of its cuisine is geared to the unadventurous palates of children, and tends to be bland and inoffensive rather than challenging. So fried chicken, steaks six ways, and ubiquitous pizzas, pastas and burgers are much in evidence. Within the theme parks, the sheer pressure of visitor numbers dictates homogenised mass catering and economies of scale rather than individually prepared dishes. Speed and convenience compensate to some extent. Even though you may have to search a little to find exceptional food in Orlando, you will rarely get a bad meal; standards of hygiene are high; service generally pleasant and efficient, and portions invariably generous. Florida's home-grown cuisine (now rediscovered for the

FOOD AND DRINK

tourism industry) is called 'cracker' cooking, and includes specialities like fried catfish, 'hush puppies' (deep-fried corn meal dough) and, what seems most outlandish of all, alligator meat ('gator tails' or nuggets), which tastes very like salty chicken. However, these homespun curiosities constitute only a tiny fraction of the vast range of ethnic and international food on offer inside and outside the theme parks. Caribbean and Cajun (Louisianian) influences are strong, particularly in gumbo (okra stew), conch chowder and many other Cajun or Creole dishes. Spanish/Mexican/Cuban flavours are imported by Florida's many Latin settlers: black-bean soup, paella, piccadillo, tacos, enchiladas, guacamole. Speciality Asian restaurants abound – Thai, Japanese, Chinese, Indian – plus of course European: Italian, Greek, French, even British. Jewish food bows in with Reubens on rye, cream cheese and lox, chicken livers and pastrami. For the health-conscious, vegetarian, organic or cholesterol-free food makes tiny inroads in the otherwise calorific and fat-laden diet that still prevails in America. Speciality desserts include Key Lime Pie and strawberry shortcake.

Eating hours blur into a steady all-day munch in Orlando. From early in the morning until late at night (all night long if you know where to look) it is possible to find just about anything you like to eat and drink. Remember, though, that you are not allowed to take food or drinks on any of the rides or attractions at WDW. Rules on alcohol are also strict: the legal age for drinking in Florida is 21, and no minors may sit or stand near a bar. No alcohol is allowed within the Magic Kingdom, but other WDW restaurants do serve it. A certain amount of wine is made in Florida but, although quite good for the most part, it does not compare favourably with Californian. Do not bother paying the expensive mark-up for imported European wines while you are there.

Breakfast

A huge range of muffins, bagels, waffles, pancakes, grits (boiled ground corn) and cinnamon toast add ballast to any sort of eggs, fruit, and yoghourt. 'Biscuits and gravy' is a strange but certainly not unpleasant concoction of savoury dough and a white sauce flavoured with sausage. Breakfast is washed down with orange juice, of course, and copious but sometimes watery coffee (you can generally have several refills).

The 'diner' or cafeteria-style restaurants often have very good inclusive deals for breakfast (often better value than hotels, or the theme park restaurants), and if you are theme-parking, it is worth stoking up early for a long hard day. If you have children to amuse, though, they will probably enjoy at least one 'character' breakfast, with Mickey and pals. On Sundays 'brunch' is a spectacular

Broiled Florida grapefruit

mid-morning banquet at several large hotels including Park Plaza in Winter Park, and WDW's Contemporary Resort and Polynesian Resort.

Lunch

Often cheaper (relatively) than dinner, so if you want a good meal, having it at midday may save you a few dollars. On the other hand, if sightseeing is your main object, spending too much time queueing and sitting in restaurants may not be a sensible use of your day. 'Grazing' (that is, munching snacks at intervals) may be a better way to satisfy your appetite. If you do want to sit down at lunchtime, make a reservation well ahead for any of the popular WDW restaurants, and try to hit them either early (before noon) or late (after 14.30hrs) to avoid the main rush. Alternatively, head for a resort hotel, or one of the less crowded Village restaurants.

Dinner

If you can eat early, before 18.00hrs, some restaurants give you a discount. There is also 'Happy Hour' to consider in many cocktail bars (see **Tight Budget** section, page 109). Dress codes are normally fairly relaxed (ties rarely required except in the very smartest restaurants), but the air-conditioning can be quite chilly, so an extra layer may be useful. Florida's summer climate makes eating out of doors an attractive option, but after dark remember the insect repellent.

Restaurant Chains

In Orlando's tourist areas you will find all the well-known franchised names: Pizza Hut, McDonalds, Wendys, Burger King, Kentucky Fried Chicken, International House of Pancakes, Baskin Robbins, Taco Bell. Chains worth looking out for include Dennys or Morrison's Cafeteria (good-value family diners), Red Lobster (seafood), Bennigan's (international snacks and steaks), Pizzeria Uno (guess what!) and Olive Garden (for reliable, mid-priced Italian food). There are any number of steakhouses: Charley's Steak House, Barney's Steak and Seafood, Cattle Ranch, and Freddie's Steak and Seafood are some of the best known.

SHOPPING

Retailing is an art form in the USA, and central Florida is a shopoholic's dream. Shops in Orlando are not mundane, practical places of commerce: they are sightseeing attractions in themselves, to some extent filling the gap left by the paucity of cultural or historic interest found in most tourist cities. Besides literally hundreds of shops devoted to the merchandising of Disney souvenirs in and around Walt Disney World, you will see countless shopping malls, markets and discount factory outlets blazoned everywhere in Orlando. Inevitably, a lot of the stuff on sale is rubbish, but never mind. You can have plenty of fun looking at it, and you may just find a real bargain. In the land of the credit card, choosing purchases may be a lot easier than paying for them. You should remember that 6 per cent sales tax is added to the marked prices (except for food bought in a grocery store).

Disney Shopping

If you have children with you it is unlikely that you will escape from Orlando without a few mementos of Mickey. First choice for kids is obviously a set of those famous ears. All over WDW, in hotels, in the theme parks, and in shopping complexes, images of the Mouse and his friends are endlessly replicated in a thousand and one guises – on T-shirts and baseball hats, pens, mugs, watches, and things you have never even thought of. If some of these souvenirs seem pretty tasteless, just wait till you get outside Walt Disney World. A word of warning on Disney shops, however. The range and scale of the eye-catching merchandise within the theme parks may distract you unduly from what will certainly be a gruelling schedule. If you spend too long browsing through the shops, you may miss out on what you really came to do, which is ride those rides. So ration yourself. If you are determined to shop, however, it is easier to do so in the mornings, before queues build. Dump any bulky purchases in the lockers by Guest Relations. There are lots of shops to visit outside the parks, so it is easy to look for souvenirs without lopping time off those rather expensive hours you spend within the turnstiles.

An excellent place to shop without paying entrance fees is **Disney Village Marketplace**, near Lake Buena Vista and the Typhoon Lagoon. This attractive complex houses well over a dozen boutiques selling high-quality souvenirs (*Open:* 10.00–22.00hrs). **Mickey's Character Shop** has the largest range of 'Disneyana' in the world. Toys depicting Disney characters and Muppets in every possible size and shape cram the shelves. Other shops specialise in glass and ceramics, jewellery, candles, or houseware. The imaginative range of stationery at Personal Message is particularly appealing. Nicely designed ink stamps make portable if not inexpensive presents. During the day (10.00–19.00hrs) the nearby shops on Pleasure Island can be visited free of charge. Try Suspended Animation for posters and lithographs, or YesterEars for nostalgia Disney. At Lake Buena Vista, opposite the Hotel Plaza is another Disney-owned shopping centre called the **Crossroads**. Here you will find more practical outlets, including a 24-hour supermarket, a pharmacy, a bank and a post office.

Shopping 'Villages'

Several complexes rival the Disney Marketplace as tourist attractions, offering restaurants and entertainment, as well as shops – in fact, functioning more or less as miniature theme parks in their own right.
Church Street Station is one of the most widely publicised of the shopping 'villages' (see also main entry, page 63, and **Nightlife**, page 102). Most of the shops are in the Exchange, a recently opened attraction with over 60 speciality shops and stalls in a glittering three-storey Victorian-style building. The shops stay open from 11.00–23.00hrs every day, plus a market (Monday–Saturday 10.00–21.00 hrs, Sunday 12.00–18.00hrs), and, unlike the other attractions within the complex, entrance to the Exchange is free. Most people visit during the evenings when the shows are on. Here the emphasis is firmly on fun shopping: magic T-shirts that change colour as you wear them, cheerfully blatant 'smellalike' fragrances, and zirconium 'diamonds'.
Park Avenue, in the smart North Orlando residential district of Winter Park, is one of the classiest places to shop. You will find names familiar in Europe among the shopfronts – Laura Ashley, Crabtree & Evelyn, Benetton. Antiques, smart bedlinen, rugs, posh toys and clothes for children, gourmet delicacies and elegant accessories are among the sophisticated offerings.

Shop with the 'stars' on Disney-MGM Studios' evocative Hollywood Boulevard

SHOPPING

Needless to say, you will need a hefty credit limit to purchase them. Most shops open at 10.00hrs.

Mercado Mediterranean Village is a Spanish-style complex on International Drive, containing over 60 shops of clothes, jewellery and ethnic crafts (Chinese pottery, Toledan daggers), with a bit of street entertainment to keep visitors amused. Shops open 10.00–22.00hrs.

Old Town, Kissimmee, on Highway 192, is a re-creation (hard to imagine in today's Orlando) of Old Florida, where over 70 shops sell a plethora of keepsakes in a setting of brick-paved streets and turn of the century architecture, plus antique carousel and ferris wheel. *Open:* daily 10.00–22.00hrs.

Shopping Malls, Factory Outlets and Flea Markets

The dividing line is fairly thin between the first two, but a mall is a bit posher. The big ones are **Florida Mall** on Sand Lake Road, **Colonial Plaza Mall** on East Colonial Drive, and **Altamonte Mall** north of Orlando. Some of these huge, charmless complexes contain upwards of 175 shops, including famous department stores like Sears and Maison Blanche.

Factory outlets claim to give discounts of up to 75 per cent, and amid a great deal of tat you can find some good buys if you can put up with the down-market atmosphere. There are several such outlets on or near **International Drive**. Luggage,

Mickey gets everywhere

cutlery, clothes, shoes, even party stationery, denim and sports equipment can be bought. One of the biggest conglomerations is the **Belz Factory Outlet Mall**, situated in the International Drive resort area, where nearly 150 discount stores can be visited. *Open:* Monday–Saturday 10.00–21.00hrs; Sunday 10.00–18.00hrs.

Another large one is the **Quality Outlet Center**. The **Dansk Factory Outlet** is widely advertised, selling well-designed Danish cookware and glass at considerable discounts. North American visitors flock to these malls and load up the car; obviously tourists from overseas have limited space in their suitcases.

Flea markets are held, usually at weekends, in several places around Orlando. There is a large one in Kissimmee, but the biggest is **Flea World** near Sanford. Hundreds of small booths sell anything and everything, and little enough you would want to buy. *Open:* Friday–Sunday 08.00–17.00hrs.

ACCOMMODATION

'Fridge and Micro. Twin Queen Beds. God is Love.' Just a sample of many motel signs whose flickering neon may temporarily distract you on the highways around Orlando. Hundreds of hotels (also referred to as 'resorts') and motels, villas, apartments and campsites now serve the millions who flock to the area each year. At the last count there were nearly 80,000 rooms available in Orlando. Many hotels concentrate on the family holiday trade, offering excellent facilities and special deals for children. Others are heavily involved in Orlando's burgeoning convention business, and are sometimes too vast and impersonal to be welcoming. Some complexes cover such acreages that electric carts are provided to get around.

While prices vary widely, depending on the facilities available, the vast majority of Orlando hotels outside Walt Disney World are unmemorable modern blocks, one very much the same as the next. The criteria for choosing one rather than another are simple: location and price. Do not expect much discernible character or individuality. Virtually all the USA's major accommodation chains are represented in Orlando, many by more than one hotel. These may be run by different franchisees, so if you have pre-booked accommodation, make sure you know the exact name and address of your hotel.

There are perhaps 16 Days Inns in Orlando, half a dozen Holiday Inns, several Howard Johnsons. Other budget or middle-range chain names you will see constantly as you travel around the area are Ramada, Radisson, Travelodge, EconoLodge, Inns of America, Economy Inns, Best Western, Comfort Inn, and Quality Inn. Sheratons, Hiltons and Marriotts are pricier, more geared to the conference market.

While many hotel or motel buildings are lamentably crude boxes of rendered cement, standards inside are generally high. Even the cheapest motel rooms have full bathrooms (showers and baths, though not bidets) and enough bedspace for four people. You can almost invariably expect a large TV with bewildering opportunities for channel-zapping, a direct-dial telephone, and air-conditioning. Pricier places may have video recorders or microwaves, while anything referred to as a 'suite' will have some kind of kitchen. Surprisingly, amid all this gadgetry, bedrooms rarely have hairdryers, except in the most expensive hotels.

Fresh-air fiends will be unhappy: most American hotel rooms are hermetically double-glazed against traffic noise, intruders, insects and the intense summer heat, and you cannot open any of the windows. Stale cigarette smoke, therefore, tends to linger even longer than usual – be sure to request a non-smoking room if this is something which bothers you.

ACCOMMODATION

Out of season (that is, any time American children are safely penned up in school), there is a surplus of accommodation, and it is always worth asking for a discount. You can get some very good deals – perhaps as little as $20 for a perfectly decent double room. Some motel chains offer free accommodation, or free meals, for children, and there are cheaper rates for senior citizens too. If you belong to the American Automobile Association (the 'Triple A'), you can get discounts in a number of chains, usually around 10 per cent.

Choosing Where to Stay

The first decision to make if Orlando is your destination is whether or not you want to stay within Walt Disney World. If you do so, you will almost certainly pay more for your holiday overall, but there are considerable advantages. With their distinctive 'themed' architecture, glossy facilities, entertainment programmes, and highly trained staff, Disney hotels aim to give guests a complete holiday experience – that is, to be much more than mere bed-factories. You also get convenient transport and access to the Disney attractions (so you will not necessarily need to hire a car), and various privileges and discounts denied to those staying outside WDW. Disney promotional literature understandably emphasises these perks, and tends to ignore any benefits of staying (indeed, of doing anything at all!) outside the site.

The attractions of Walt Disney World are so many and varied that some visitors are quite content to spend all their holiday just doing Disney things. On the other hand you may find yourself wondering what goes on beyond the compound. Walt Disney World is by no means all that Orlando has to offer, and if you plan to stay longer than a week you may need a rest from Mickey and his little friends.

If you choose to stay outside WDW, you will almost certainly need a car (even if you stay on site, a rental car is highly recommended). Even the hotels advertised as 'right next to the Maingate entrance' are still miles away from the theme park turnstiles, so huge is the Disney complex.

Staying within the Walt Disney World resort

Within the confines of this vast theme park complex lie some eighteen large hotels (two new ones are due to open in 1992). Several of these function as self-contained resorts. Most of these hotels are actually owned and run by the Disney organisation; others (the World Dolphin and World Swan, and the seven on the Hotel Plaza near the Village) are leased or owned by other companies, but run strictly in accordance with the Disney ethos, right down to the receptionists' nail-polish! Alternative WDW accommodation consists of a large group of villas (Village Resort), and a camping ground called Fort Wilderness covering 780 acres (316 ha). See

Camping in the **Directory**,
page 114.
All the Disney properties are
extremely comfortable,
imaginatively designed and
pleasantly located in spacious,
beautifully landscaped
grounds. Needless to say, these
luxury properties are not
cheap, and high-season prices
are awesome. None the less,
most Disney accommodation is
fully booked during peak
holiday periods.

Staying outside WDW
Accommodation outside Walt
Disney World is concentrated in
two main areas. Highway 192,
which runs east-west past the
southern Maingate entrance to
Walt Disney World towards the
community of Kissimmee, is
packed with hotels and motels.
It is a noisy, busy road, and the
development along it, as along
most highways in Orlando, is
hardly picturesque. The further
away you are from Walt Disney
World, the cheaper the tariffs,
so if you are prepared to drive

The Grand Floridian Beach Resort

a few miles you can certainly
pick up a good bargain along
here, especially out of season.
Most of the other
accommodation lies north-east
of Walt Disney World, in the
corridor of the main Interstate
Highway (I-4) which runs
directly (usually uncongested)
towards downtown Orlando.
There is a large concentration
of hotels along International
Drive, just east of I-4 – with its
numerous attractions, a popular
and convenient area to stay.
Others lie further east on Sand
Lake Road, the Orange Blossom
Trail, and around the
international airport. From these
areas there are quite a few
traffic-laden miles to drive to
reach WDW.
There is plenty of
accommodation in central
Orlando too, mostly in
unexceptional if perfectly
comfortable business hotels.
But the advantages or
attractions of staying hemmed

ACCOMMODATION

in by buildings this far from the main sights are very limited – except perhaps in high season, when lower prices and occupancy rates may be worth considering.

Further afield, a couple of hotels are appealing and unusual enough to consider as more than merely a bed for the night. One is in Winter Park, north of Orlando (Park Plaza), the other in Lakeland to the west, near the Cypress Gardens (Chalet Suzanne). See page 101, **Treats outside Orlando**, for details of these two.

Accommodation inside Walt Disney World

Resort Hotels and Villas

All Disney hotels are recommendable for their facilities and high standards of comfort. But they all have a different feel, and a different price tag – high, or very high! Cheapest rates are available at the Caribbean Beach Resort, and the new Port Orleans and Dixie Landings Hotels. Individual room-rates vary depending on the view, rather than the quality of the facilities. Location is also a consideration, though wherever you stay within Walt Disney World, efficient free transport is available.

Three of the four Magic Kingdom resort hotels lie on the shores of the Seven Seas Lagoon, and are conveniently linked by the monorail system. These are the Grand Floridian Beach, the Contemporary, and the Polynesian Resorts. The smaller Disney Inn lies a little way south-west in a quiet oasis

of golf links and woodland. The EPCOT Center resorts are the Caribbean Beach, the Yacht Club and Beach Club, and the World Dolphin and World Swan. Disney Village resorts include the suite hotel (Village Resort), plus Disney's two newest resorts, Dixie Landings and Port Orleans, both opened in 1992 (not yet inspected). These recreate Old South themes – New Orleans' French quarter and the Mississippi plantations. The Mediterranean (with a Greek-island theme) is the next planned resort. There are seven other, more traditional, hotels nearby (see Hotel Plaza, page 98). For advance bookings at all these properties, contact **WDW Central Reservations**, Box 10000, Lake Buena Vista 32830, tel: 407-W DISNEY (934 7639).

Grand Floridian Beach Resort (tel: 824 3000). Victorian-looking turrets, gables and bargeboards characterise this rambling, red-roofed complex. Striking features include a soaring five-storey lobby, where colossal chandeliers hover beneath domes of stained glass, and rare birds twitter in an aviary. Big Bertha, a fairground organ, regales visitors in one of the restaurants.

Contemporary Resort (tel: 824 1000). This vast concrete A-frame structure catches the eye (rather excessively) all round the Magic Kingdom. The monorail disappears inside it, dropping visitors off right by the lobby. Some find the architecture and style of this hotel alienating. Inside, the multi-storey car park atmosphere wears off gradually; the vertiginous heights of the atrium dwindle into people-scale compartments, and the decor is certainly imaginative. Many bedrooms are in low-rise garden wings outside the tower block.

Polynesian Resort (tel: 824 2000). South Pacific motifs prevail. Visitors check in at the Great Ceremonial House, where tropical vegetation drips into a maze of pools and fountains. 'Longhouses' named after exotic islands stretch round the grounds, oddly drab with their brown, corrugated-iron-look roofing. At night, the gardens come alive with flaming gas torches, and lilting 'luau' music wafts across the soft white-sand beaches.

Disney Inn (tel: 824 2200). A smaller, quieter hotel rather out on a limb. Some prefer its peaceful rustic setting between two golf courses. There is less bustle than in other Disney resorts, but your chances of meeting golf addicts are pretty high. Decor lacks the determined eccentricity of other hotels, and is somewhat bland.

Caribbean Beach Resort (tel: 934 3400). A very extensive complex made up of a confection of separate, prettily designed, low-rise 'villages' (Aruba, Barbados, Jamaica, Martinique and Trinidad), each rendered in a different colour, with its own pool and little artificial lake-beach. Check in at the colonial-style Custom House, shop in the Calypso

Trading Post or dine in a food-court at Old Port Royale. Lots of entertainment and an island play area for kids. Cheerful staff redirect you when you are lost. One of the most attractive and best-value Disney hotel properties.

Yacht and **Beach Club Resorts** (tel: 934 7000 and 934 8000 respectively). These two hotels effectively function as one, though they do have distinct 'themes'. Externally the only difference between their Eastern Seaboard architecture is the colour: oyster-grey for the Yacht Club; harebell-blue for the Beach Club. The Yacht Club goes for nautical décor inside, all brass rails and gleaming mahogany; the Beach Club is a slice of old New England, clapboard and clam chowder. A particularly nice feature is the waterfront and white-sand beach, and a fantasy lagoon inside a mock shipwreck, where you can swim alongside freshwater fish, or hurtle down waterslides.

World Swan and **World Dolphin Hotels** (tel: 934 3000 and 934 4000 respectively). Though leased and operated by two different companies (Westin and Sheraton), these magnificently eccentric buildings were simultaneously designed both inside and out by the architect Michael Graves, and are very similar in size and concept. They now make eye-catching twin landmarks all around EPCOT. As fantastic externally as anything in Walt Disney World, their bold facades look like painted film-sets, one all waves

ACCOMMODATION

and giant swans, the other graced by a vast shell waterfall tumbling down its side, huge urns and 55-foot (17-metre) dolphins. Inside, the fantasy continues with Egyptian motifs, pineapples, and monkey chandeliers. Like them or not, in a world of standardised construction these hotels are a breath of fresh air.

Village Resort (tel: 827 1100). Five well-equipped types of villa are available on this extensive site near the Marketplace, sleeping from four to six adults. They range from one-bedroomed Vacation Villas to the luxury Grand Vista Suites or the intriguing Treehouse Villas on stilts in a pinewood. Facilities and furnishings are of a very high standard, and for families of 5-plus they represent an interesting option. Lots of sports amenities are available on site, including golf, swimming, tennis, fishing and boating. To get around you can hire bikes or electric carts, or use the free bus network. The Gourmet Pantry provides groceries (free delivery service).

Hotel Plaza

The other group of hotels within WDW lies to the east, in the section called Walt Disney World Village. Along the Hotel Plaza Boulevard stand seven large hotel blocks. Guests who stay here enjoy the same privileges as other Disney clients, such as free use of the transport system throughout the parks, priority bookings for dinner shows, use of Village Clubhouse sports facilities, and so on. The hotels are the gleaming tower-block Buena Vista Palace, the Grosvenor Resort, the Hilton, the Howard Johnson Resort, the Royal Plaza, a Travelodge and a massive suite complex known as the Guest Quarters. These are the two we liked best:

Hilton, 1751 Hotel Plaza Boulevard, Lake Buena Vista (tel: 827 4000 or toll free 800 782 4414). This wide-angled slab of concrete looks somewhat daunting from outside. It is, of course, smoothly geared to the business executive trade, with many state-of-the-art facilities and prices to suit. But it caters well for families with children too: Hilton's Youth Hotel's supervised programme is available to take them off your hands for a while. Public areas are bland but user-friendly. Good-value self-service buffet.

Grosvenor Resort, 1850 Hotel Plaza Boulevard, Lake Buena Vista (tel: 828 4444 or toll free 800 624 4109). Easily one of the most attractive and personal hotels in this complex, with an agreeable mix of family and corporate trade. Though less expensive than the Hilton, it is no budget option, but its excellent location and views, comfortable bedrooms and friendliness of staff make it one of the best value. Decor is handsome: a vaguely 19th-century colonial feel in pastel shades. A special feature is the Sherlock Holmes museum in one of its restaurants, a recreation of 221B Baker Street, London – legendary home of Sir Arthur Conan Doyle's famous sleuth.

Accommodation outside Walt Disney World

International Drive Area

Expensive

Peabody Orlando, 9801 International Drive (tel: 352 4000). This daunting high-rise hotel stands in spacious grounds at the classier, southern end of 'The Drive'. More appealing than the lavish interior and predictably luxurious facilities are its impeccable standards of service and friendly, personal attention. The Peabody's most winsome feature, though, is an unexpected tribe of resident mallards. Every morning, at 11.00hrs, a drake and his four wives waddle before their keeper along a red carpet to splash away the day in the marble lobby fountain, then march back again at 17.00hrs. The Duck March has now achieved the status of a local tourist attraction. If you can afford it, this is a fine hotel to be pampered in. If not, at least go and say hello to the ducks!

Sonesta Villa Resort, 10,000 Turkey Lake Road (tel: 352 8051). This well spaced, low-rise complex stands west of the I-4, just a few minutes drive from Walt Disney World, in quiet lakeshore surroundings. Its tastefully designed, pantiled townhouses are screened from road noise and each other by palms and fountains. The site's excellent facilities include watersports and whirlpools, a full programme of activities for children, and well-equipped kitchenettes. A grocery delivery service is available.

Moderate

Orlando Heritage Inn, 9861 International Drive (tel: 352 0008). Rockers on the front porch lend an air of relaxed southern hospitality to this attractive, plantation-style hotel next to the Peabody. Inside, brass chandeliers, dark wood fittings and paddle fans evoke the charm of 19th-century Florida, and bedrooms have colonial touches. Theatre dinners feature several times a week in the big circular dining hall. The Golden Tulip connection makes it a popular venue for Dutch guests. A complimentary shuttle bus takes you to the attractions.

The Peabody Orlando

ACCOMMODATION

Delta Orlando Resort, 5715 Major Boulevard (tel: 351 3340). Low-rise blocks, functional but unobtrusive, stand in peaceful, spacious grounds just a stone's throw from Universal Studios (complimentary shuttle). Bedrooms show signs of wear in places, but the pool terrace, adventure playground, and mini-golf course are pleasant, staff are friendly, and the tariff is very good value.

Inexpensive
Comfort Inn International, 5825 International Drive (tel: 351 4100). Though the location is a busy intersection at the drearier north end of the street, there is a surprisingly rustic flavour to these two-storey motel blocks with wooden balconies and shutters, set round a small, neat pool. The newer bedrooms, while not luxurious, are quite stylish. Plenty of nightlife and restaurants lie within easy reach, including the good facilities of the Star Quality Resort just across the road.

Highway 192

Moderate
Ramada Resort Maingate, 2950 Reedy Creek Boulevard, Kissimmee (tel: 396 4466). One of the closest off-site hotels to Walt Disney World, this unobtrusive building shows no great promise from outside, but is quietly set back from the main highway overlooking the woodlands of WDW and its own small gardens and pool. Decor (pale blue rattan and blondwood in public areas; tasteful modern fabrics in

bedrooms) is light and inoffensive; rooms are spacious and well equipped. In common with several hotels close by, a free shuttle bus service operates regularly to WDW.

Holiday Inn Maingate West #2, 7601 Black Lake Road, Kissimmee (tel: 240 7100). Check the address and your compass (close by there is also a Holiday Inn Maingate, and a Holiday Inn Maingate East – all, incidentally, run by different companies!) for this pink-washed building set back from Highway 192, less than two miles (3km) west of WDW's main entrance. As with many local hotels, its box-like exterior belies the high standards of furnishings within and its general air of quietness. Staff are helpful; the plant-filled foyer lounge and Palms restaurant cool and relaxing.

Holiday Inn Maingate, 7300 Irlo Bronson Memorial Highway, Kissimmee (tel: 396 7300). Though the roadside block opposite WDW's Maingate entrance looks uninvitingly close to the highway, its large, tasteful bedrooms are well insulated, and rear rooms are right away from the traffic. Do not necessarily expect a quiet life, however: this hotel caters particularly for families with children, with stacks of entertainment, playgrounds and paddling pools, and child-oriented fast food.

Sol Orlando, 4787 West Irlo Bronson Memorial Highway, Kissimmee (tel: 397 0555). Spanish-style villas in a secluded, attractive complex well back from the road. Public areas (a well-furnished lobby and restaurant) have more personality than most, and the pantiled bedroom wings are comfortable and civilised.

Inexpensive

Casa Rosa Inn, 4600 West Irlo Bronson Parkway, Kissimmee (tel: 305–396 2020). More hacienda overtones in this pink-washed, family-run motel. Facilities are limited, and there may be the faintest burr of traffic noise in some rooms, but the atmosphere is notably friendly and welcoming: the coffee-pot is always on by reception, and free videos are available to watch in bed. Plenty of restaurants and nightlife all around.

Treats outside Orlando

Park Plaza, 307 Park Avenue South, Winter Park (tel: 647 1072). One of very few hotels in Orlando that counts as intimate, personal, and genuinely classy. In an up-market residential suburb of North Orlando, the hotel overlooks Central Park and the smart shopping street of Park Avenue. No two of its 27 rooms are the same, though all are decorated and furnished with equal panache. Antiques and oriental rugs grace bedrooms festooned with plants, whirling fans and white wickerwork. Outside some of these elegant, comfortable rooms runs a balcony where you can take your complimentary continental breakfast amid fern-laden hanging baskets. Staff are unfailingly helpful and courteous, and the food in the

Every comfort at Chalet Suzanne

Gardens restaurant is something to remember (see **Restaurants**, page 78).

Chalet Suzanne, US27S (exit 17A), Drawer AC, Lake Wales 33859 (tel: 813 676 6011). You find this unusual restaurant and country inn in Orlando's Lakeland, as you head for the Cypress Gardens or the Bok Tower Gardens. This whimsical Florida mansion seems to have stepped out of some gentle, old-fashioned Disney animation, its 30 charmingly folksy bedrooms scattered through a village-like complex of cottages and mini-castles. Opened during the Depression by its enterprising, newly widowed doyenne, Chalet Suzanne is now a smart enough venue to require a private landing strip in its lake-and-woodland grounds amid the citrus groves. The gourmet food is a strong point: well worth a trek for dinner in its elegantly cluttered restaurant even if you are not staying here (see **Restaurants**, page 75).

NIGHTLIFE AND ENTERTAINMENT

Entertainment in Orlando does not stop as darkness falls, but, like the rest of the region's attractions, it is very much geared to families and is almost always wholesome enough for the most sensitive child or maiden aunt. The big theme parks (Magic Kingdom, EPCOT Center, Sea World and Universal Studios) end the day with some kind of spectacular pageant. The attractions of Church Street Station and Pleasure Island really come to life in the evenings, though the shops and restaurants stay open all day (for details, see the separate entries). Dinner shows and evening cruises are tourist-circuit staples, and many hotels and restaurants provide live entertainment of some sort. For discos, head downtown to **J J Whispers**, on Lee Road. You can find rock and roll at **Little Darlin's**, off US192, in Kissimmee. Winter Park boasts a few chic bars and clubs for the smart set, such as the Crocodile Club at **Bailey's Restaurant** (West Fairbanks Avenue), and **Sullivan's Trailways Lounge** is a good place for dancing. Pick up the local newspaper, the *Orlando Sentinel*, for weekly 'what's on' listings, or *Center State*, a monthly arts magazine with a calendar of events. Ballet, opera and dance companies and orchestras perform seasonally on tour. Orlando's main theatres are at **Loch Haven Park**, and **Rollins College**, Winter Park.

Walt Disney World Nightlife

The Disney folk hang on to their customers as long as possible by ending each day at the parks with a loud bang: fireworks and lasers in EPCOT Center; a water pageant and a parade of brightly lit electrical floats bearing Disney characters in the Magic Kingdom. Both these regular events are very colourful and exciting for children, and it is worth staying till closing time to catch them. Disney's specialist nightspot is **Pleasure Island**, near the Village, a waterfront stage-set of wharfs and warehouses where New Year's Eve is celebrated nightly with a continuous whoopee of shows and disco dancing (more fully described on page 48). Several 'official' Disney hotels in the Village (see **Hotel Plaza**, page 98) have nightspots: the **Buena Vista Palace** has a flashy nightclub called the Laughing Kookaburra; the **Royal Plaza** has the Giraffe Lounge disco and La Cantina guitar bar; the **Grosvenor** offers murder and mystery evenings in its Sherlock Holmes themed restaurant, Baskervilles, and the Moriarty pub. Dinner shows are regularly held at several Disney resorts, the most popular of which is at Fort Wilderness. Book up quickly if you want to catch the *Hoop-Dee-Doo Musical Revue* at the Pioneer Hall in Fort Wilderness, a sort of giant log cabin. Audiences munch through a hefty meal of honeyed corn, barbecued spare ribs, baked beans, chicken pieces and strawberry shortcake, interspersed with

Country and Western song and dance routines and corny wisecracks. The enthusiasm of the entertainers is infectious and astonishing, considering they do the same show three times a night (at 17.00, 19.30 and 22.00hrs) to packed houses. Dress casual.

The Contemporary Resort's Top of the World restaurant on the 15th floor provides a smart, formal setting for a pretty good dinner and *Broadway at the Top* – a big band medley of hits from great Broadway shows of yesteryear (Andrew Lloyd Webber plays a significant, unacknowledged part). No marks for originality, but snazzy costumes, good dancing and lots of pizazz.

The Polynesian Revue is a gentle South Pacific 'luau' show down by the white-sand tropical cove of the Polynesian Resort, with music, flower garlands, native hula dancing, and a barbecue. It is a nice but not particularly gripping event,

incidentally rivalled by Sea World's similar evening cabaret. An afternoon show at 16.30hrs called *Mickey's Tropical Revue* brings Disney characters into a south-sea context for the children.

Dinner Shows outside WDW

Among the showers of leaflets advertising Orlando's attractions you are bound to encounter news of these popular nightly spectacles, often included in holiday packages.

King Henry's Feast, held in a mock-Tudor palace, 8984 International Drive (tel: 351 5151), is one of the best-paced and most entertaining of these uproarious themed dinner shows. Diners sit round a raised dais from which the king and his jester select a lucky seventh, or even an eighth prospective 'wife' from the audience. Wenches serve the chicken joints and spare ribs

Everyone's a performer, it seems

NIGHTLIFE AND ENTERTAINMENT

Catastrophe Canyon, on Disney-MGM's Backstage Studio Tour

and endlessly flowing drink; sword-fighting knights, jugglers and minstrels keep the show rolling. The acts are well rehearsed, the jester amiably impertinent, the king a great showman.

Arabian Nights, 6225 West Irlo Bronson Memorial Highway, Kissimmee (tel: 239 9223). Scheherezade searches for her prince in an enormous arena covered in wood-chip fibre, but the stars of this show are the Arabian and Lippizaner horses who perform dancing and leaping acrobatics. The programme includes a Ben Hur chariot race, a superb black stallion, and a prime-rib dinner. Some acts need more rehearsal, but this show is well liked by many visitors.

Medieval Times A Spanish-style pageant of horsemanship, falconry, swordplay and jousting in a fake castle on Highway 192, Kissimmee (tel: 396 1518). Audience participation approaches deafening levels as their chosen knights compete on classy Andalucian horses, and distribute carnation favours. The jousting acts are impressively performed, and the roast chicken dinner (eaten with your fingers, of course) appetising.

Other dinner shows widely advertised include a Wild West-style romp at **Fort Liberty**, 5260 Highway 192, Kissimmee (tel: 351 5151); a carnival scene at **Mardi Gras**, The Mercado, 8445 International Drive (tel: 351 5151); an Oriental evening at **Asian Dynasty**, 5225 International Drive (tel: 354 0880); a whodunnit mystery show called **Sleuths**, 7508 Republican Drive (tel: 363 1985); and a steamboat cruise on the *Grand Romance* rivership, based in Sanford (see page 79).

Most of these evening entertainments are quite expensive ($25–30), and the food suffers the fate of most mass catering, but try at least one while you are there.

WEATHER AND WHEN TO GO

During the summer (late May to September), midday temperatures in central Florida soar into the mid-30sC (90sF), accompanied by intense humidity and thunderous rainstorms. The rest of the year the heat is more bearable, somewhere in the 16–21°C (60sF) or mid-20sC (70sF), though night-time lows can sink into the 10–15°C (50sF), and, as those withered citrus groves around Orlando indicate, quite severe winter frosts are not unknown. Temperatures inland are more variable than on the Florida coast, which is tempered by the Gulf Stream. On the other hand, the violent hurricanes that sometimes batter coastal districts during the late summer have usually moderated to ill-tempered squalls by the time they reach Walt Disney World, and serious storm damage is rare. The wettest months in Orlando are June, July, August and September, which, combined with the heat, can be quite oppressive. It is dryest from November to January. Early morning fog can present a hazard to drivers at certain times of year.

What to Wear

If you visit Orlando during summer, take precautions against the sun. Queueing for rides in those temperatures is no joke, and it is particularly important to keep an eye on young children, who quickly wilt in the heat. Wear a hat and an effective sunscreen, even in the winter months, whenever you are spending long periods outside. Take a light cagoule or folding umbrella with you into the parks; almost every afternoon in summer the blue skies blacken for a brief but thoroughly drenching shower. Whenever this happens a flurry of bright yellow Mickey ponchos miraculously appears on every Disney shop counter for the foolish virgins who have left their raincoats in the car park.

Dress codes in Orlando are casual, with comfort being the prime consideration. Loose cotton T-shirts, shorts, and trainers may not suit everyone, but you will quickly discover why the vast majority of American visitors virtually live in this relaxed garb while exploring the theme parks. Too much stripping off, however, is frowned on: quaint notices at Walt Disney World inform visitors that shirts and shoes are

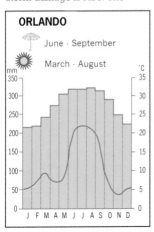

ORLANDO

June · September

March · August

obligatory. At any time of year, take a light jacket or sweater for cool evenings, or over-zealous air-conditioning. Smarter hotels and eating places may insist that men wear a jacket, though ties are rarely required. By far the most important item of clothing to take, however, is a pair of thoroughly comfortable shoes. You will spend many hours regretting it if you don't!

When to Go

Ideally, avoid the American school holidays. This may not be practical advice if you have children of school age, but Walt Disney World becomes hideously overcrowded at Easter, Christmas and New Year, and the major public holidays such as Thanksgiving (3rd week in November), Washington's Birthday (mid-February), and of course 4 July. Any time from mid-June to late August is also more than usually crowded with families, as is the spring break in late March. From Christmas to Easter, the winter season, Florida's mild weather attracts long-stay visitors from northerly states, many of whom have second homes in Florida. Special events, such as space launches, also attract a sudden influx of visitors. Late spring and autumn (April/May, or October to mid-December) are good times to go: crowds are lighter, queues shorter, accommodation cheaper and easier to book, and temperatures much pleasanter for exploring. During quiet times, however, you may find some of the attractions closed for renovation, and the parks shut early, without the colourful evening parades and firework shows.

Oddly enough, tourist patterns in the USA mean that weekends are not the most crowded days in the parks. In fact, Fridays and Sundays are quietest of all, Thursdays and Saturdays quite good, and Mondays, Tuesdays and Wednesdays the busiest. Whichever day you go, however, get to the parks early – at least half an hour before the official opening time – and make the most of cooler, quieter mornings for the most popular rides.

HOW TO BE A LOCAL

All you need to do to mesh with central Florida is relax, abandon inhibitions, and have a nice day! Orlando is not for the standoffish or painfully shy, or for those seeking meaningful cultural experiences. Just about everyone there is some sort of tourist, so everything is geared towards you, and towards having a continuous round of rollicking, childish fun. Native Floridians are naturally easy-going and friendly, and the pace of life is southern and slowish. Add to that the polished smiles of Walt Disney World's employees, and you would have to be churlish indeed to feel unhappy. Just one note of caution: Florida is a tolerant but conservative place, and behaviour that offends the respectable sensibilities of family-oriented Middle America is out. That includes stripping off by the pool, public drunkenness and drug abuse.

CHILDREN

Most of this book is dedicated to children – that is, to the child in all of us. Parents pretend they are taking their offspring to Orlando's theme parks, but they emerge from the rides grinning like jackasses, unwilling to admit how much they have enjoyed themselves. Walt Disney World caters magnificently for children of all ages, as do most of Orlando's attractions, hotels and restaurants.

Child-care facilities at Walt Disney World and the other main theme parks include playgrounds, games rooms, crèches and day-care centres, name tags (in case they get lost), strollers (pushchairs) rentable for $4–5 a day, nappy-changing and feeding rooms, baby-sitters, cots, bibs and high-chairs, and a large stock of all kinds of baby equipment, books and toys on sale. There is an efficient, vigilant system of rounding up children who have strayed, and Mickey and his friends are constantly on hand to entertain and cheer up their young fans. Guest services desks in all the parks can give information about facilities for children.

The Stress Factor

You have paid a lot of money, travelled a long way, and your expectations are somewhere in orbit. The children are excited, and terribly overtired. You have bought a pass for an arm and a leg, but you only have a few days to spare, and there is an awful lot to see. The queues look awesome, and the sun beats down. Somehow, you must fight your way in and enjoy yourselves. Just the time for trouble. No sooner through the turnstiles, and the wails begin. The size and scale of Orlando's attractions can place a lot of pressure on small children – and their keepers. Rule one, get them in a good frame of mind before you start. Keep things relaxed and low key. You may plan the day with military precision, but don't convey this to the kids. Make an early start, but don't worry if

A holiday for children of all ages

everyone needs a break at some point. Have lunch, or leave the parks altogether and go back to your hotel for a swim and a rest if it is not too far – you can return later if you get a hand-stamp of invisible fluorescent ink as you leave. Check the individual entries in this book for approximate guidelines on how suitable individual attractions are for different age ranges. It is impossible to predict children's reactions accurately, however. They may take the wildest roller-coaster completely in their stride, then become strangely alarmed at some innocuous fibreglass monster.

Meeting Mickey
A visit to Walt Disney World would not be complete without at least one close personal encounter with Mickey.The best place to find the Disney characters is Mickey's Starland, in the Magic Kingdom, but you will see them during afternoon parades too (best viewpoint is Frontierland), or catch them over 'Character breakfasts' at several of the resort hotels.

Education or Entertainment?
Despite worthy enterprises such as EPCOT Center, the educational element at Walt Disney World and the other theme parks is limited. Children are too bombarded with sensations to take in much information. So if you have taken your children out of school to visit Orlando, don't fool yourself they are learning a lot. It's fun, great fun, but not much else.

TIGHT BUDGET

Orlando throbs with temptations to spend money at every turn, and it is painfully easy to let more dollars trickle through your fingers than you anticipated, particularly if you have impulsive children in tow. Some things are relatively inexpensive by European standards: petrol, car hire, food and accommodation – if carefully chosen. But that 6 per cent sales tax (nearly always added on top of the prices displayed, except essential food items), and the pointed reminders that gratuities (usually between 15 and 20 per cent) are not included in the bill, can make unexpected dents in your budget. In addition, a resort tax of between 2 and 4 per cent is levied on hotel bills.

● Visit Orlando out of high season, when package prices, hotel costs, car hire and entrance charges may be much lower. Ask for a discount if your hotel is plainly not full. Competition is fierce at slack periods.

● Prioritise attraction visits carefully. Decide what you want to see and do in the time available, and stick to your plans. Some of Orlando's minor diversions represent poor value for money.

● Car hire costs vary widely, and local dealers may be cheaper than big international companies. Collision damage waiver and adequate insurance are essential, but the gold-plated insurance cover some companies try to sell you is very expensive, and generally unnecessary (see **Driving, page** 115).

● Choose accommodation carefully; you will pay for posh facilities, whether you use them or not. Remember that most bedrooms sleep at least four people, and the price stays the same. If you have a large party, consider renting a villa or condominium.

● Some hotels and restaurants (especially the chains) offer special deals for children (they stay or eat free), or senior citizens, but age limits and periods of application vary. Some hotels offer discounts of around 10 per cent to members of the American Automobile Association. Check also the free tourist newspapers and leaflets, which often contain worthwhile discount coupons.

● Use tea- and coffee-making facilities in hotels, and the ice machines for supermarket cold drinks, rather than constantly paying bar and restaurant prices.

● Avoid expensive telephone calls from hotel bedrooms. There is often a 75 per cent mark-up on long-distance calls, and that is not very far in Orlando – the region spans three separate counties.

● Meal portions are nearly always very generous. Order just one course to start with, and see how hungry you are afterwards. Lunches in smarter restaurants are usually less costly than dinners; or you could skip lunch altogether and have a hefty brunch.

● Many cocktail bars have a 'Happy Hour' somewhere

The Python, Busch Gardens

between 17.30 and 19.30hrs. Drinks are half-price, with enough free canapés and snacks to stave off evening hunger pangs.

● Diners, fast-food chains and self-service cafés are more economical places to stoke up than big hotels. Look out for inclusive 'all-you-can-eat' prices, and cheaper 'early bird' dinner menus before 17.00 or 18.00hrs.

● Cut down on the incidentals: snacks, ice-creams and souvenirs soon mount up with a family.

● Shop at factory outlets such as Belz, or markets such as Flea World (see **Shopping**, pages 90–92).

● While it is important not to dehydrate in Florida's hot sunshine, repeated rounds of soft drinks are expensive and calorific, and may cause stomach chills. Make use of the drinking-water fountains liberally placed throughout the big theme parks. They are hygienic, fast, unfattening – and free!

● There is a premium on stamps if you buy them from a slot machine, though you see these everywhere. Get them from post offices (rather few and far between), or Walt Disney World hotels.

● A word of warning on booths selling 'discount' Walt Disney World tickets. These are very often a front for time-share dealers, and you may be inveigled into inspecting some property or other.

● Two of Orlando's main through-routes (the Beeline Expressway and Florida's Turnpike) are toll roads. The only time you really need them is if you are dashing for a plane, or hammering off to Miami. The I-75 is a useful alternative north–south route, rather than the Turnpike, and will also take you to Miami.

Spills at the Silver Spurs Rodeo

SPECIAL EVENTS

Central Florida's energetic tourist carousel revolves with a year-round programme of festivals, sports events and party celebrations, especially at holiday times. It is easy to find out what is going on from local newspapers, free visitor guides and stacks of promotional leaflets fluttering around hotel lobbies and other public places. For more details or reservations, contact guest relations staff at tourist hotels and theme parks, or the Orlando/Orange County Convention and Visitors Bureau at 8445 International Drive (in the Mercado Mediterranean Village, tel: 363 5871). Some of the main regular annual fixtures are listed below.

January
New Year Celebrations, Walt Disney World; Florida Citrus Bowl Football Classic, Orlando Stadium; Scottish Highland Games, Central Florida Fairgrounds.

February
Disney Village Wine Festival;Black Hills Passion Play, Lake Wales; Central Florida Fair, Central Florida Fairgrounds; Silver Spurs Rodeo, Kissimmee (also takes place in July).

March
Houston Astros Spring Training (baseball), Osceola County Stadium, Kissimmee; Kissimmee Bluegrass Festival; Nestlé International PGA Tour (golf), Bay Hill Club; St Patrick's Day Street Party, Church Street Station; Winter Park Sidewalk Art Festival.

April
Orlando Sunrays baseball season begins (April–August); Easter Parades at WDW.
May
Up, Up and Away Airport Art Show, Orlando International Airport.
June
Kissimmee Boat-a-Cade, Lake Tohopekaliga.
July
Silver Spurs Rodeo, Kissimmee; Fourth of July Celebrations, WDW.
September
Osceola Art Festival, Lake Toho (Tohopekaliga), Kissimmee; Oktoberfest (really!), Church Street Station; Autofest, Old Town, Kissimmee (classic cars).
October
Pioneer Days (folk festival), Pine Castle Folk Art Center; Florida State Air Fair, Kissimmee; Kissimmee Boating Jamboree, Lake Toho; Oldsmobile Golf Classic, WDW; Hallowe'en celebrations throughout Orlando.
November
Festival of Masters (art show), Disney Village Marketplace; Light Up Orlando (street party), downtown Orlando.
December
Pet Fair, Loch Haven Park; Half-marathon, Lake Eola Park; Christmas Celebrations, WDW.

SPORT

Sports facilities are an important aspect of central Florida's status as a complete holiday playground. Those available at Walt Disney World alone are impressive enough, but outside Mouseland there are stacks

All-weather courts are available

more. Orlando's vast number of lakes and rivers provide a venue for inland watersports, but should you crave salt and surf it is only an hour or so's easy drive to either coastline. Tuition and equipment hire are easily arranged; bring suitable clothes. For more information, phone the **Orlando Recreation Department** on 363 5871.

Golf Walt Disney World has five courses of its own: two near the Disney Inn by the Magic Kingdom, two near the Dixie Landings Resort, north-east of EPCOT Center, and one at Lake Buena Vista. Green fees for these mid-range championship courses are quite expensive, even for Disney guests. There is also a six-hole course by Lake Buena Vista. An important annual event (for spectators unless you are very keen and very rich) is the WDW/ Oldsmobile Golf Classic tournament in October. Within easy range of Orlando are at least eight other golf resorts.

Tennis The Contemporary Resort, with six floodlit courts, is a good bet for keen tennis players, but several other WDW resort hotels have hard courts (lessons can be arranged). Outside WDW, half a dozen centres have multiple all-weather floodlit courts, many free of charge.

Fishing Bass-fishing is one of central Florida's most popular sports. Bay Lake and the Seven Seas Lagoon in WDW permit strictly controlled two-hour fishing trips (no licence required). Fishing is free (and again no licence is required) in the waterways around Fort Wilderness Resort. If you have cooking facilities you can keep your fish; otherwise you just chuck the poor things back in for the next punter. Lots of other fishing camps organise trips, especially on Lake Toho, Kissimmee. A licence is required on all other Florida waters – for more information about fishing in the area, contact the regional office of the **Florida Game and Fresh Water Fish Commission**, 3900 Drane Field Road, Lakeland, FL 33811 (tel: 813 648 3202).

Watersports Many varied craft can be hired for use on WDW lakes: tiny powered water sprites, pedal boats, outrigger canoes, motor boats and sailing boats. One of the nicest watersports centres in Walt Disney World is River Country (see page 50). Outside WDW, several rural spots for camping, swimming and canoeing lie north of the city, along the Wekiva River. Whizzier watersports in Orlando include waterskiing, parasailing, boardsailing, and airboats (try Splash 'N' Ski, Ski Holidays, or

Airboat Rentals). Luxury houseboats are available for hire on the St John's River. Most hotels in Orlando have some sort of swimming pool, whether it be a little motel puddle in hard, hot concrete, or the elaborate three-tiered fantasy at the Hyatt Regency Grand Cypress, complete with grottoes and waterfalls. If you are mad on swimming, head for WDW's beautifully landscaped Typhoon Lagoon (see pages 49-50), the high-tech tubular water-parks of Wet 'n Wild and Water Mania (see page 82), or the Radisson Inn Aquatic Center on International Drive.

Riding You can ride gentle, unthreatening mounts (age limit, 9 plus) at Disney's Fort Wilderness, more excitingly along old logging trails at Poinciana Horse World (tel: 847 4343) in Kissimmee, and several other stables.

Other Sports Ice-skating, bowling, jogging and cycling can also be arranged. Spectator sports include a Jai Alai centre and a dog-track north of Orlando, the Orlando Magic Basketball team, several baseball teams, and, of course, American football. Perhaps the most exciting sporting activity, available in several locations, is hot-air ballooning. Trips are not cheap, at around $150 per person, but the sight of these colourful craft slowly drifting across Orlando's dawn skyline is enchanting. Rosie O'Grady's Flying Circus (tel: 407 841 UPUP) at Church Street Station is one of the most widely advertised companies, offering champagne breakfast trips.

Directory

This section (with the biscuit-coloured band) contains day-to-day information, including travel, health and documentation

Contents

Arriving
Camping
Crime
Customs
  Regulations
Disabled People
Driving
Electricity
Embassies and
  Consulates
Emergency
  Telephone Nos

Entertainment
  Information
Health
Holidays
Lost Property
Media
Money Matters
Opening Times
Personal Safety
Pharmacies
Places of Worship
Police

Post Office
Public Transport
Senior Citizens
Student and Youth
  Travel
Telephones
Time
Tipping
Toilets
Tourist Offices
Travel Agencies

Arriving

Orlando's international airport is one of the fastest growing in the US, handling over 18 million passengers annually, and around 800 flights a day. It is currently undergoing a massive $800 million expansion programme which will eventually give it four terminals and runways. It is an efficient and pleasant airport, with an enterprising range of restaurants. Souvenir shops from the major theme parks give visitors a first chance to buy Mouse Ears and, needless to say, there is a Walt Disney World information centre. Over 50 airlines fly into Orlando, including scheduled flights with British Airways, Delta, North-West, TWA, Eastern, KLM, American, US, and Continental, plus many charters such as Virgin, Britannia and British Airtours. Florida's alternative airports are at Tampa, about an hour and a half's drive away from Orlando, or Miami (about five hours). From Orlando's airport, take the Beeline Expressway westwards for Walt Disney World or International Drive, where most tourists stay. It is a toll road, so have a couple of dollars of loose change handy. It is a bus route (costing around $10 single as far as International Drive); taxis are much more expensive ($35 or so). Some major hotels provide a complimentary shuttle service (others charge for it).

Travel Documents Many foreign visitors with a valid return ticket no longer require a visa to enter the US for stays (business or leisure) not exceeding 90 days. All you need is a passport (British Visitors' Passport not acceptable). You may need a visa if you plan to leave the US at any point during your stay, such as a visit to Mexico or the Caribbean. Check with the US Embassy before you leave. You must complete a visa waiver form, which will be processed at your first entry point to the US. If you take a connecting flight, have your form ready for your first encounter with US immigration authorities, who like things in apple-pie order.

Camping

The great outdoors is as popular in Florida as anywhere in the States, and there is plenty of opportunity in and around Orlando for all kinds of year-round camping, whether in a simple tent, an 'RV' (Recreational Vehicle) or static trailer home with all mod cons. Walt Disney World devotes a huge 650-acre (263-ha) resort, **Fort Wilderness**, to camping, offering over 800 wooded sites for tents, RVs and luxuriously kitted Fleetwood Trailers with air-conditioning and huge TVs. There are stacks of sports, shops, and things to do on site. Alternatives include three widely advertised **Yogi Bear's Jellystone Park** sites, Fort Summit's Western-style campground at **Baseball City**

(I-4/US27 interchange) and the lakeside **Port 0' Call Campground** in Kissimmee. All these are large, with the sort of facilities that obviate any pressing need to experience nature at first hand. Simpler, more backwoodsy options can be found in the attractive Wekiva River area north of Orlando (log cabins to rent), or in Lakeland, to the west. The *Florida Camping Directory*, an annual publication, is available free from Florida Campground Association, Department D-8, 1638 North Plaza Drive, Tallahassee, FL 32308-5323 (tel: 904 656 8878). The American Automobile Association (AAA) also produces a list of camping grounds.

Chemist see Pharmacies

Crime

Orlando is pleasantly relaxed and relatively free of the sort of crime likely to affect tourists. Money escapes from your pockets in lots of quite legitimate ways; otherwise, it is more likely to fall out as you are upside-down on a roller-coaster than anything else. Take obvious, sensible precautions: never carry too much loose cash; use hotel safes (usually provided free of charge to guests); lock and bolt your motel door. Miami's rich pickings have attracted many opportunist thieves, and if you plan a coastal excursion, be very vigilant. Get a good map and never stray into unsalubrious downtown sectors. The police, tourist office, or AAA can advise you on no-go areas.

Customs Regulations

Non-US residents aged 21 or over can bring in up to a litre of alcohol; 200 cigarettes or 50 cigars (or 100 non-Cuban cigars) and gifts worth up to $100. There are no currency limits. Regulations on importing meat products, seeds or plants are very strict. That Cox's Pippin you packed for the connecting flight will be humourlessly confiscated with a stern reprimand. Just imagine what they do with narcotics!

Disabled People

The major theme parks, particularly Walt Disney World, score very highly for their thoughtful provision of facilities for elderly and disabled visitors. All but the wildest rides are accessible, and highly trained, friendly staff are always on hand to help. Wheelchairs can be rented inexpensively in all the parks for anyone who has difficulty in walking, and wheelchair visitors are always given priority in queues; most restrooms (WCs), car parks, lifts and entrances are sensibly planned. Audio and visual aids are available for sight- or hearing-impaired visitors. A free booklet, *The Disabled Guest*, is available from Walt Disney World (tel: 824 4321).

Driving

Americans drive on the right, calculate distances in miles, and buy petrol (gas) in US gallons (slightly smaller than the imperial measure). The road system all around Orlando is excellent, with well-maintained four- and six-lane highways in all directions. Even so, the

Downtown Orlando

sheer volume of visitors can clog them up at peak periods, and there is a significant rush-hour factor in downtown Orlando. The most useful road in Orlando is Interstate Highway 4, known as I-4, which runs from Tampa on the west coast of Florida to Daytona on the east. It is a fast, painless artery bypass through Orlando and the International Drive area to Walt Disney World where most of the attractions lie. Exits are clearly marked. Get to know them, and be compass-literate – you need to know if you are heading east or west. A couple of highways in Orlando (the Beeline Expressway (SR528) leading to the airport, and the north–south Florida's Turnpike) are toll roads – avoid these unless you are in a special hurry. An alternative north–south route, rather than the Turnpike, is the I-75. Driving techniques in the US are different from those in Europe. Most vehicles proceed sedately, sticking to the (fairly low) speed limits, constantly in the same lane. You can overtake on either side, but unnecessary lane-hopping is ill advised. Sometimes extreme right- or left-hand lanes are for exit traffic only, so it is best to avoid these until you need them. Note that you are permitted to turn right on red if it is safe to do so, unless a sign indicates otherwise. STOP for school buses unloading, or you will be fined. Always park the same way round as passing traffic. One thing that may confuse non-US visitors is that overhead street signs indicate *intersections* (the street at right angles, *not* the street you are actually driving on). Speed limits vary from as low as 20mph (32kph) in residential streets to 65mph (104kph) on open freeways. It is generally 55mph (88kph) on highways, and these limits are quite strictly enforced. Sometimes there is a minimum limit, too. Watch out for 'Florida Ice', a mix of water and oil during rain showers that creates extremely slippery driving conditions. Petrol (gas) is still very cheap in the US by European standards, and comes in three grades, all unleaded (about $1.10 a gallon for the cheapest, suitable for a compact car). At gas stations, you have a choice of serve yourself (slightly cheaper), or be served, and perhaps get your windows cleaned at the same time. Some stations have automatic vending machines that accept notes.

Car Rental

Life in the US is highly geared to the motorist, and if you want to do any degree of exploring it is best to have the use of a car. Car hire in Orlando is a good bargain; rates are very competitive, and several tour operators offer such excellent fly-drive deals that it is worth fixing a car up before you arrive. Alamo Rent-a-Car, Dollar, Thrifty and Lindo's are popular agencies used by tour operators, and all the big international firms (Hertz, Avis, Budget) are represented in Orlando. Best rates are weekly, not daily. Make sure you have an unlimited mileage deal, and take out collision damage waiver, along with adequate (that means more than minimal) insurance. Some firms, besides trying to upgrade the car you have booked, will attempt to persuade you to take out massively high insurance cover, which could add as much as 50 per cent to your bill. This is not necessary; nevertheless, bear in mind that many drivers in the US are inadequately insured, and that it is a notoriously litigious society. The reasonably priced 'top-up' cover recommended by some operators is well worth considering for peace of mind. Some car-rental firms impose a surcharge on drivers under 25, and the minimum age is often 21 (Hertz's limit is 18). Some deals do not allow you to drive outside Florida and Georgia. Visitors from some countries need an International Driver's Permit, and many firms expect you to pay by credit card (see

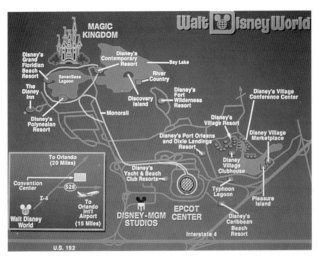

A map will help you plan your time

Money Matters, page 120). A 'compact' car is the smallest – OK for two, but take something bigger if you have a family and lots of luggage. Nearly all rental cars in the US are automatics, so try to disregard your left leg. They are very easy to get used to, and about as much fun to drive as a milk-float. Air-conditioning is a standard feature, and one you will be glad of in summer.

The Triple A

The American Automobile Association (AAA) provides certain reciprocal membership facilities to affiliated motoring organisations in other countries, such as the AA. These do not include discounts on accommodation, restaurants or attractions, but their touring guides, routeing and general motoring advice, emergency road rescue – and above all their excellent 'Triptik' strip-maps (most other maps of

Orlando are abysmal) – are well worth having. The AAA's Orlando office is the national HQ, at Heathrow, heading north of Orlando just off Highway I-4 (Junction 50, Lake Mary Boulevard). Take proof of membership with you, obviously. **American Automobile Association**, 1000 AAA Drive, Heathrow, FL 32746–5063; tel: 444 8202. For emergency roadside assistance, ring 1-800-824 4432 (toll-free).

Electricity

In the US the current is 110–120 volt AC as opposed to the 220-volt current in use in Europe. Plugs have two small flat pins, and foreign appliances without dual voltage will need both a transformer and an adaptor, otherwise an adaptor alone will suffice. If in doubt, ask at your hotel.

DIRECTORY

Embassies and Consulates

Australia: 636 Fifth Avenue, New York (tel: 212-245 4000).
Canada: 1251 Avenue of the Americas, New York (tel: 212-586 2400).
Republic of Ireland: 515 Madison Avenue, New York (tel: 212-319 2555).
United Kingdom: 1001 South Bayshore Drive, Miami (tel: 374 1522).

Emergency Telephone Numbers

Dial 911 for all emergency services, or ask the operator (0) to help you.

Entertainment Information

All over Orlando in hotel lobbies and other public places you will find racks of free

Disney parks have internal transport

leaflets and visitors' guides galore advertising local attractions. Many holiday hotels have a special guest services desk where you can book any trips or shows. Walt Disney World is splendidly efficient at disseminating information about its own attractions, and understandably more reticent about rival happenings in Orlando (tel: 824 4321). The local newspaper, the *Orlando Sentinel*, gives events listings on Fridays. *Orlando Magazine* has 'Time Out' coverage of museums, galleries, and local events. (See also **Tourist Offices**, page 126.) Some 'tourist information' booths offering free or discount tickets are actually time-share sellers hoping to persuade you to see (and buy) a property.

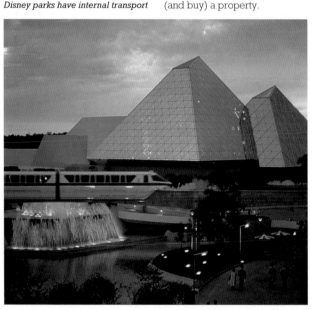

Health

No inoculations are specifically required for Florida, but it is as well to check with your doctor before leaving. It is, however, a rabies zone. If you happen to be bitten or scratched by any mammal, wild or domesticated, get medical attention. There have also been several outbreaks of a nasty viral infection called St Louis encephalitis during the last few years. This is carried by mosquitoes. Try to avoid bites by using a good insect repellent containing DEET (diethyltoluamide), and keeping skin covered after dark. By far the most common source of ill health in Florida, however, is too much sun. Wear a hat and sun-screen while you are outside, and make sure that small children take in enough fluid. Minor ailments can be handled by the first aid stations in all the big theme parks. **The Family Treatment Center**, at 6001 Vineland Road (tel: 351 6682), or the **Buena Vista Walk-in Medical Center**, near WDW Village (tel: 828 3434) are useful. There is a home visit service for hotel guests called **HouseMed** (tel: 648 9234). A convenient hospital in the area is the **Orlando Regional Medical Center**, 1414 South Kuhl Avenue (tel: 841 5111), or the **Sand Lake Hospital**, 9400 Turkey Lake Road (tel: 351 8500). It is very important to make sure that you are adequately insured for any trip to the US, since medical bills can be astronomical, and treatment may simply be withheld if you have no

Don't neglect Orlando's other treats

evidence of the means to pay. A policy offering at least $1,000,000, and preferably unlimited, medical cover is recommended.

Holidays

1 January, New Year's Day; third Monday in January, Martin Luther King's Birthday; third Monday in February, Washington's Birthday; March/April, Good Friday; last Monday in May, Memorial Day; 4 July, Independence Day; first Monday in September, Labor Day; second Monday in October, Columbus Day; 11 November, Veterans' Day; fourth Thursday in November, Thanksgiving Day; 25 December, Christmas Day.

DIRECTORY

Lost Property

The theme parks, especially WDW, are highly organised about lost and found items, including children (name tags; lost children's logbooks). Head for **City Hall** in the Magic Kingdom; **Earth Station** at EPCOT Center, and **Hollywood Boulevard Guest Services** in Disney–MGM Studios. Incidentally, if no one claims an item at WDW, it's finders keepers, so it could be worth being a good citizen and handing something in. Report serious losses to the police or you will not be able to make an insurance claim. Take advantage of the safe deposit boxes at hotels; they are free or very cheap.

Media

Dozens of radio and TV stations bemuse the visitor more or less round the clock. Whatever home comforts your motel does or doesn't have, it will most certainly possess an enormous TV set. Despite the apparent range, there is little enough to choose between most networks; watching or listening in the US is usually an irksome process of channel-zapping through a maze of inferior pop, B-movies and game shows to avoid the commercials. The Public Broadcasting Service shows a more interesting range of programmes and has better news coverage than most. Many motels and hotels feature videos, but you may have to pay extra to hire these, or to watch cable TV. The most widely available local newspaper is the *Orlando Sentinel*, delivered free to guests in the smarter hotels. You can buy other US national papers in many places, and foreign newspapers too, but the mark-up is high.

Money Matters

It is best to take the bulk of your currency in US dollar traveller's cheques ('checks' in America), including plenty of smallish denominations ($10 or $20). These are widely accepted like ordinary currency in petrol stations, hotels, restaurants, shops, etc, and are, of course, more secure than loose cash. You do not, therefore, need to keep running into banks; in any case, these are not thick on the ground in Orlando, and those that do exist do not generally serve the tourist's *bureau de change* needs. An exception is the **SunBank** (there are several branches in WDW), which can cash and sell traveller's cheques, provide refunds for lost cheques, give cash advances on credit cards, help wire money transfers, etc. You can also exchange foreign currency at lots of places in WDW, including resort hotels, and guest services windows. Beware poor exchange rates in non-Disney hotels. A well-known credit card is one of life's necessities in the US ('Cash or charge?', they'll ask when you pay).

One surprising feature of US currency is that all the notes of whatever denomination are exactly the same size and colour – all greenbacks. So check the numbers. 25¢ (quarters) and 50¢ (half-dollar)

Choose your own theme holiday

coins are useful for telephone calls, toll roads, buses, stamp machines (but see **Post Office**, page 123). Single dollar bills are handy for tips (an all-pervasive US custom). The 6 per cent sales tax added to practically everything in Florida results in curiously irregular final bills, which means your pocket or purse rapidly silts up with pennies (1¢), nickels (5¢) and dimes (10¢). At some point you will have to think of a way of disposing of these.
Visitors to Walt Disney World will encounter another sign of the Mouse's might: Mickey

even has his own currency.
Disney Dollars are fun for kids.
They can be obtained from
ticket booths, guest relations
and resort hotels, and can be
used to purchase food or
souvenirs anywhere within
WDW. There is no mark-up on
them, and they are redeemable
for greenbacks at any time.

Opening Times

SunBanks are generally open
from 09.00 to 16.00hrs Monday
to Friday (closed at weekends).
The branch at Orlando
International Airport is open
Monday–Friday 08.00–
18.00hrs, Saturday 08.00–
17.00hrs. Many shops do not
open before 10.00hrs, but do
not shut till 18.00hrs or so,
Monday to Saturday. Most malls
and shopping centres,
however, are open Monday–
Saturday 10.00–21.00hrs,
Sunday 12.00–18.00hrs. Theme
park shops follow the park
opening hours.
Major theme park opening
times vary greatly, depending
on seasonal demand, and may

change at short notice. In high
season they open early
(generally from 08.30hrs), and
stay open late, sometimes till
midnight. But check carefully
during your stay, or you could
be caught out. (See also page
20.) Some museums close on
Mondays. Post Offices usually
open Monday–Friday 09.00–
17.00hrs,but many hotels and
major attractions provide a post
office service for longer hours.

Personal Safety

Orlando is not generally a
dangerous place. So far, the
major theme parks have kept
an admirable safety record,
particularly Walt Disney World.
But accidents are not unknown.
Particular attention should be
paid to all warning notices and
announcements (keeping your
hands and arms clear of moving
equipment, not jumping from
car to car, etc). These are, after
all, thrill rides, and as such
entail certain hazards. Do not
do the scary things (such as

Sorcery in the Sky

Space Mountain) if you are pregnant, or if you have a bad back or neck – if in doubt, check with your doctor before leaving. G-force stresses are very noticeable on some rides. Motion sickness and dizziness are obvious contra-indications, though few rides last long enough to cause many problems.

Alligators are found in fresh water everywhere in the state, and are extremely dangerous – do not feed or molest them in any way. Although rarely aggressive unless they are bothered, they can come out of the water and outrun a horse over a short distance. Never allow small children or pets to approach an alligator *under any circumstances*, and do not swim if alligators are present. If you are bitten, even by a very small alligator, seek medical attention immediately.

Pharmacies

You can buy simple medicaments at any drug store, though certain drugs generally available elsewhere require a prescription in the US. Acetaminophen is the US equivalent of paracetamol. A couple of downtown pharmacies (**Ekerd Drugs**, 908 Lee Road; **Walgreen Drug Store**, 2410 East Colonial Drive) stay open all night. Holiday hotels, particularly in WDW, can always help out with a plaster or aspirin.

Places of Worship

WDW caters for multifarious creeds. Protestants can head for Luau Cove at the Polynesian Village (Sundays at 09.00hrs);

Catholics get in earlier (at 08.00hrs), or later (at 10.15hrs). Check with guest services. There are plenty of churches (Baptist, Presbyterian, Methodist, you name it) all over Orlando, and a couple of synagogues too (liberal and conservative). If you are into spiritualism, head for Cassadaga (see page 79). The *Orlando Sentinel* gives details of church services on Saturdays.

Police

Dial **911** if you want them. If you don't, stick to the speed limits and don't drink and drive – the penalties for drink-driving offences are severe. In this tourist-oriented region, however, the police are friendly and courteous towards foreigners, and fairly tolerant of minor misdemeanours or confusions.

City police deal with local crime; the Highway Patrol deal with traffic violations and look out for motorists stranded by the roadside. Pull over, raise the bonnet lid and put your hazard lights on if you are in trouble.

Post Office

They do exist (there is a useful one at the Lake Buena Vista Crossroads shopping center in WDW), but are thin on the ground; a request for stamps is generally met by a wave towards a vending machine. Besides requiring vast amounts of small change, these charge a 25 per cent premium. It is best to buy them at the reception of any WDW resort hotel, or the information offices (e.g., **City Hall** in The Magic Kingdom) of the big parks (see also **Opening Times**, page 122).

Public Transport

Air

Orlando is now a major routeing hub. You can fly non-stop to Orlando from about 50 different US cities, on over a dozen airlines (see also **Arriving**, page 113).

Bus

Greyhound Lines serve Orlando from many centres in the US; within the metropolitan Orlando area, local buses provide a good service, notably the **Gray Line**, which serves the airport and most of Orlando's main attractions and hotels (tel: 422 0744). Many hotels have their own courtesy buses, and WDW has an entire fleet of efficient, clearly flagged buses whirling constantly around, all completely free for resort guests (see page 21).

Rail

AmTrak serves Orlando, also stopping at Winter Park and Sanford north of the city, and Kissimmee near WDW (for general information, tel: 800 872 7245, toll-free).

Taxi

These are too expensive ($2.25 for the first mile, $1.30 for each additional mile) to be a sensible option for anything other than occasional or short-distance hops, but if money really is no object, limousine transport can easily be arranged through your hotel's guest services desk.

Senior Citizens (Seniors)

Florida attracts huge numbers of elderly visitors and permanent residents, many of whom feel young enough at heart for a trip to Walt Disney World. Saga International Holidays, a specialist operator for the elderly, has a package programme to Orlando. AARPs (American Association of Retired Persons, over 50) are eligible (with ID) for discounts on accommodation, meals, car rental, transport, and many of the attraction charges in the Orlando area; other discounts are available for the over 60s. Staff at WDW and other theme parks should be able to help with any special needs.

Student and Youth Travel

While it is true that most concessions at the major theme parks apply to children (under 17), some attractions and sights offer special admission prices for bona fide students, and there are also concessionary rail fares (International Student Identity Card as proof).

Telephones

Available in lots of public places (hotel lobbies, drug stores, restaurants, garages and at the roadside). You need 5¢, 10¢ or 25¢ coins (local calls usually cost 25¢, but local calls from some of the small private telephone companies' phones may cost $2 or more). For **assistance** dial the operator (0). For local directory enquiries, dial 411. 'Collect' means reverse the charges. Orlando spans several telephone areas, and calling Walt Disney World from downtown is long-distance. The area code for Orlando is 407.

For **long-distance** within the area code, dial 1 plus the number. Outside the area code, dial 1, plus code, plus number. Note that long-distance calls from hotel rooms attract a high mark-up.

Cheap rates apply after 17.00hrs, even cheaper between 23.00 and 08.00hrs. Many hotels, airlines, attractions, etc, have toll-free (free of charge) numbers for potential customers – look out for numbers beginning with 800.

To call abroad from the USA, dial 011 plus the country code (44 UK; 353 Eire; 1 Canada; 61 Australia; 64 New Zealand), the area code minus the initial '0', then the number. For the USA from abroad, dial 101 1 and the area code (407 for Orlando) and the number.

Main Street, USA and Cinderella Castle in Walt Disney World

Time

Local time is Eastern Standard
(same as New York), which is
five hours behind GMT.
Daylight saving applies, with
clocks an hour ahead between
April and October. A note on
dates: the US convention is
month/day/year (thus 13
December 1991 = 12.13.91).

Tipping

Definitely a feature of the
democratic egalitarian society.
Customers are forcefully
reminded that *Gratuities Are
Not Included* as they stump up
for a meal, though in some
places a service charge is
automatically added. Staff rely
heavily on tips to make a
decent living. At Walt Disney
World, however, staff do not
hover for tips, and indeed are
not permitted to accept them in
the fast-food restaurants, but as
elsewhere it is customary in
restaurants with table service
(between 10 and 20 per cent).
However, attractions that
feature dinner usually include
gratuities, and no extra is
required. Cabbies expect
around 15 per cent; porters 50¢
a bag (a dollar is the minimum
you can decently proffer).

Toilets

Known euphemistically as 'rest
rooms' in the US, also as 'the
men's/ladies' room', more
excruciatingly as 'comfort
stations'. In a private house, you
would ask for the 'bathroom'.
They are nearly always well
kept, and free.

Tourist Offices

The Orlando/Orange County
Convention and Visitors'
Bureau has an **information
centre** in the Mercado
Mediterranean Shopping
Village at 8445 International
Drive (tel: 363 5871; open: daily
08.00 to 20.00hrs), where you
can pick up stacks of leaflets
and brochures about what's on,
including the free *Visitor's
Guide*, plus discount tickets to
area attractions and theme
parks. There is another centre
at **Kissimmee**, 2.5 miles (4km)
east of I-4 on US192, at 1925
East Irlo Bronson Memorial
Highway, PO Box 2007,
Kissimmee, FL 32742 (tel: 847
5000).
Disney operates its own vastly
efficient network of information
centres all over the world: in
Britain contact the **Walt Disney
Company Ltd**, 31–32 Soho
Square, London W1V 6AP (tel:
071-734 8111). The *Walt Disney
World Vacation Guide* is a
useful compendium of
information.
For pre-trip information from
the UK, contact the **Orlando
Visitors' and Convention
Bureau**, 182–194 Union Street,
London SE1 0LH (tel: 071 261
9438), the **US Travel and
Tourism Administration**, PO
Box 1, London W1A 1EN (tel:
071 439 7433), or the **Florida
Division of Tourism**, 18–24
Westbourne Grove, London W2
5RH (tel: 071 727 1661).

Travel Agencies

Almost any large holiday hotel
will have a guest services desk
with information on car hire,
local attractions, reservations,
etc. Offices advertising tours
and tickets can be found in all
the main visitor areas.

INDEX

Acknowledgements

The Automobile Association wishes to thank the following photographers, libraries and associations for their assistance in the preparation of this book: **Busch Gardens** 65 crocodiles, 109 Python roller coaster; **Chalet Suzanne** 89 grapefruit, 101 Chalet Suzanne; **Church Street Station** 63 Church Street Station, 67 dancer, Church Street Station; **Kennedy Space Center** 68 Rocket Garden, 71 IMAX screen; **The Morse Moseum of American Art** 77 Tiffany window; **Nature Photographers Ltd** 83 Green Heron, 84 alligator, 86 Egret (all by Paul Sterry); **Orlando/Orange County Convention & Visitors Bureau** 119 citrus fruits, 121 sunset; **The Peabody Hotel** 99 Peabody Hotel, 111 tennis courts; **The Riverside Grand Romance** 78 Grand Romance; **Silver Spurs Rodeo** 110 Rodeo; **Universal Studios Florida** 12 Universal Studios, 56 Earthquake, 60 Wild West Stunt Show; **© The Walt Disney Company 1992** *cover* Parade, 5 Fantasyland, 6 Mickey , 7 Big Thunder Mountain, 8 Hollywood Boulevard, 10 Wonders of Life, 11 World Showcase, 14 Spaceship Earth, 15 MGM Studios, 21 Caribbean Beach, 22 Mickey, 23 The Living Seas, 27 Journey into Imagination, 28 Wonders of Life, 29 China Pavilion, 30 Living Seas restaurant, 33 Fireworks from Main Street, 34 Haunted Mansion, 39 Space Mountain, 41 Great Movie Ride, 42 Earffel Tower, 45 Animation building, 47 Star Tours, 48 River Country, 51 Typhoon Lagoon, 91 Hollywood Boulevard, 92 Mickey, 95 Grand Floridian Hotel, 103 Living Seas, 104 Catastrophe Canyon, 107 Giant Bee, 117 Walt Disney Properties, 118 Epcot, 122 Sorcery in the Sky, 125 Main Street.
The remaining photographs are held in the **AA Photo Library** with contributions from: Pete Bennett.